Memeology:
History of Your Favorite Memes

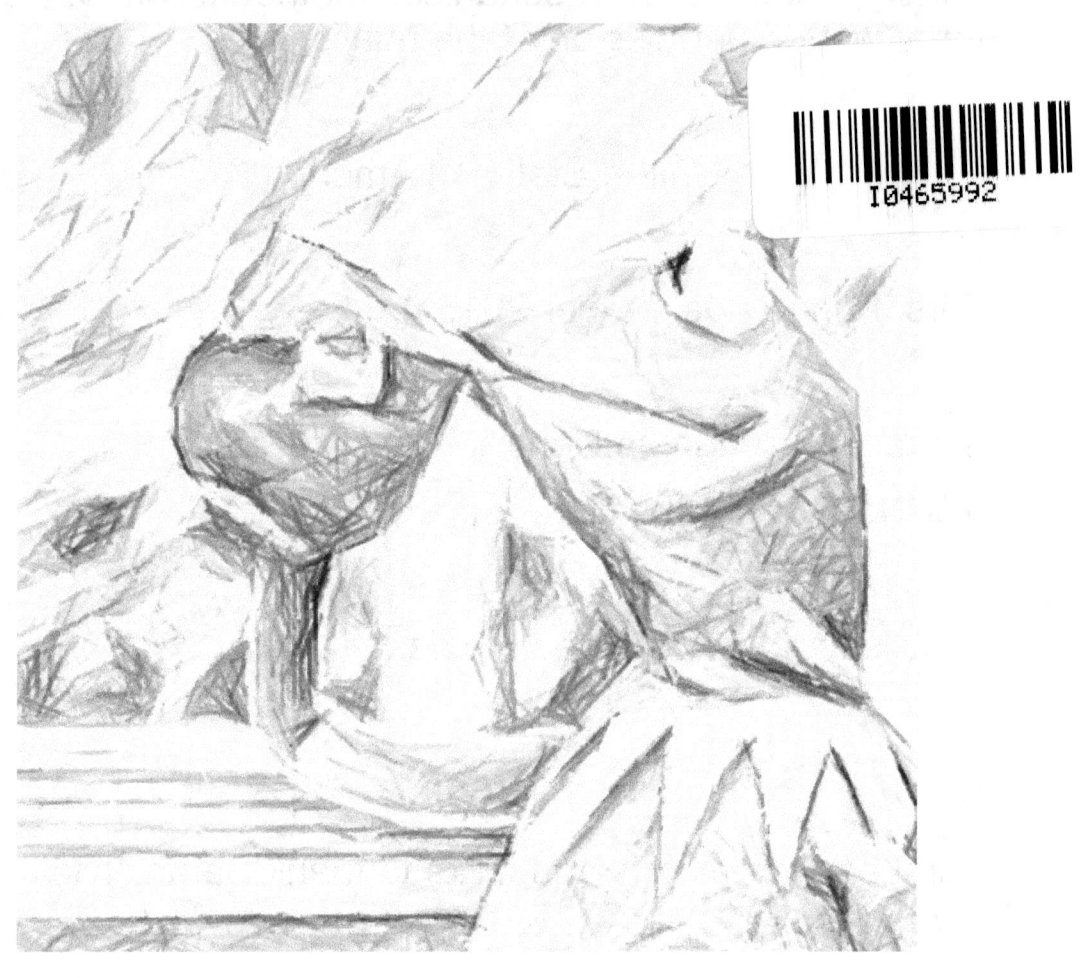

Adult Coloring Book

By: D.A.B.

Printed in the United States of America

First Printing December 2018

Library of Congress Control Number: Pending
ISBN: 9781791934149

Published by: Boss Idea Media

Credits

First and foremost I would like to thank Satan, The Dark Lord!

Totally Kidding!

This book is dedicated to its true creator, the people of the internet. Without the millions of daily users and everyday amateur comedians, the memes and meme culture we know and love would not exist.

Table of Contents

Memeology

The term 'Meme' originates from the Greek word mīmeîsthai which means 'to imitate or copy'. Today, memes are an essential part of popular culture. They are simplistic images, gifs, and videos that we use to cleverly critique the human condition.

The purpose of the Memeology History (and Adult Coloring) Book is to document the origins of some of the most pervasive images and inside jokes on the internet.

This is an academic and humanitarian effort. Written documentation of meme culture will be important 5 million years from now when historians are attempting to decipher why humans had access to limitless knowledge yet decided to look at randomly captioned images.

The answers to which are both simple and complex:

Because they are more relatable than any one person could comprehend.

And because they are funny…..

ENJOY!

Surprised Pikachu

The "Surprised Pikachu" meme took the internet by storm in 2018. The image is originally from Season 1, Episode 10 of the animated series Pokémon.

The meme is commonly used to express confusion at the consequences of a situation that anyone could have seen coming. Who would have thought that actions had consequences?

Teacher: We will have a pop quiz next class.

Teacher gives pop quiz next class

Me:

When I bend something fragile and it breaks into pieces.

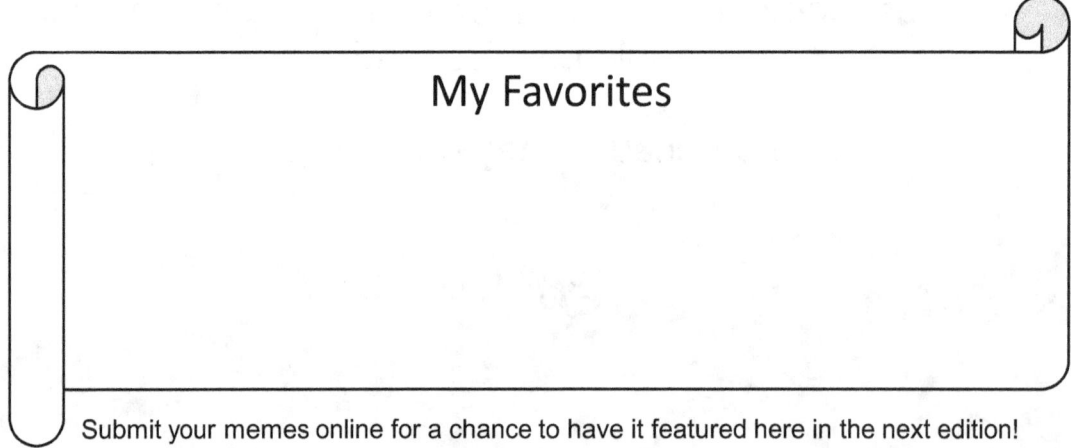

My Favorites

Submit your memes online for a chance to have it featured here in the next edition!

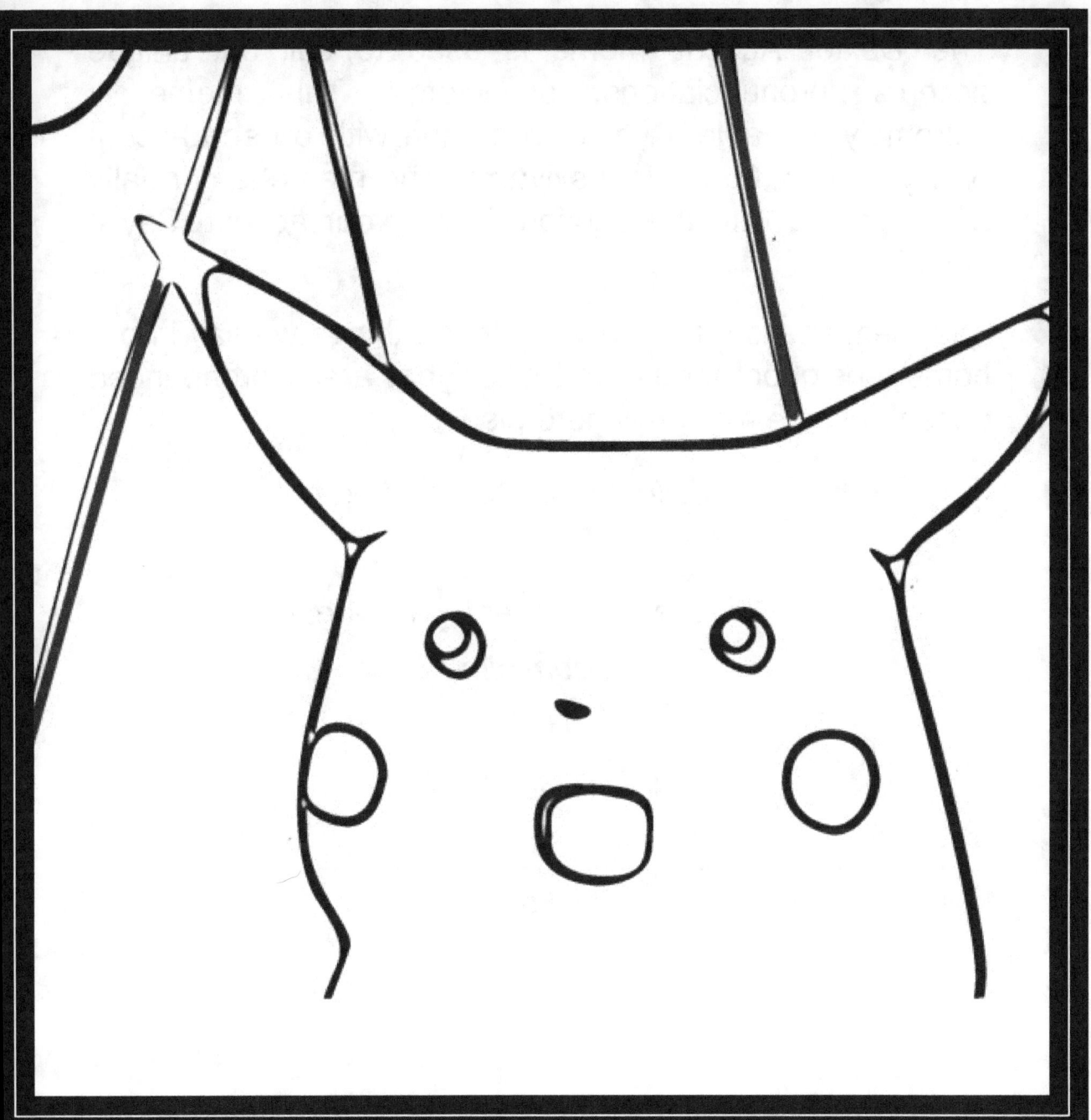

Memeology

Dexter's Accent

The 'Dexter Accent' meme is used to call out unique accents, pronunciations, or idioms. This meme is extremely relatable if you're a person with a deep accent or if you grew up in Pennsylvania. The meme is normally accompanied with the caption 'I love your accent. Say it again!'

The meme calls attention to all those things we say in our homes, neighborhoods, and cities that aren't pronounced quite the same way anywhere else.

It's in da worshama sheen

I love your accent, say it again.
"Loominim Foyl"
"Hell Nawl"
"Car Warsh"

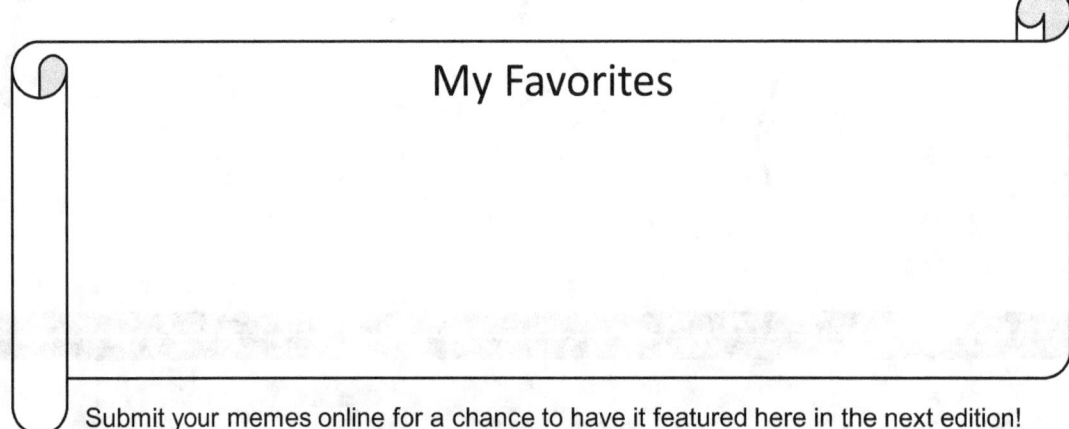

My Favorites

Submit your memes online for a chance to have it featured here in the next edition!

4

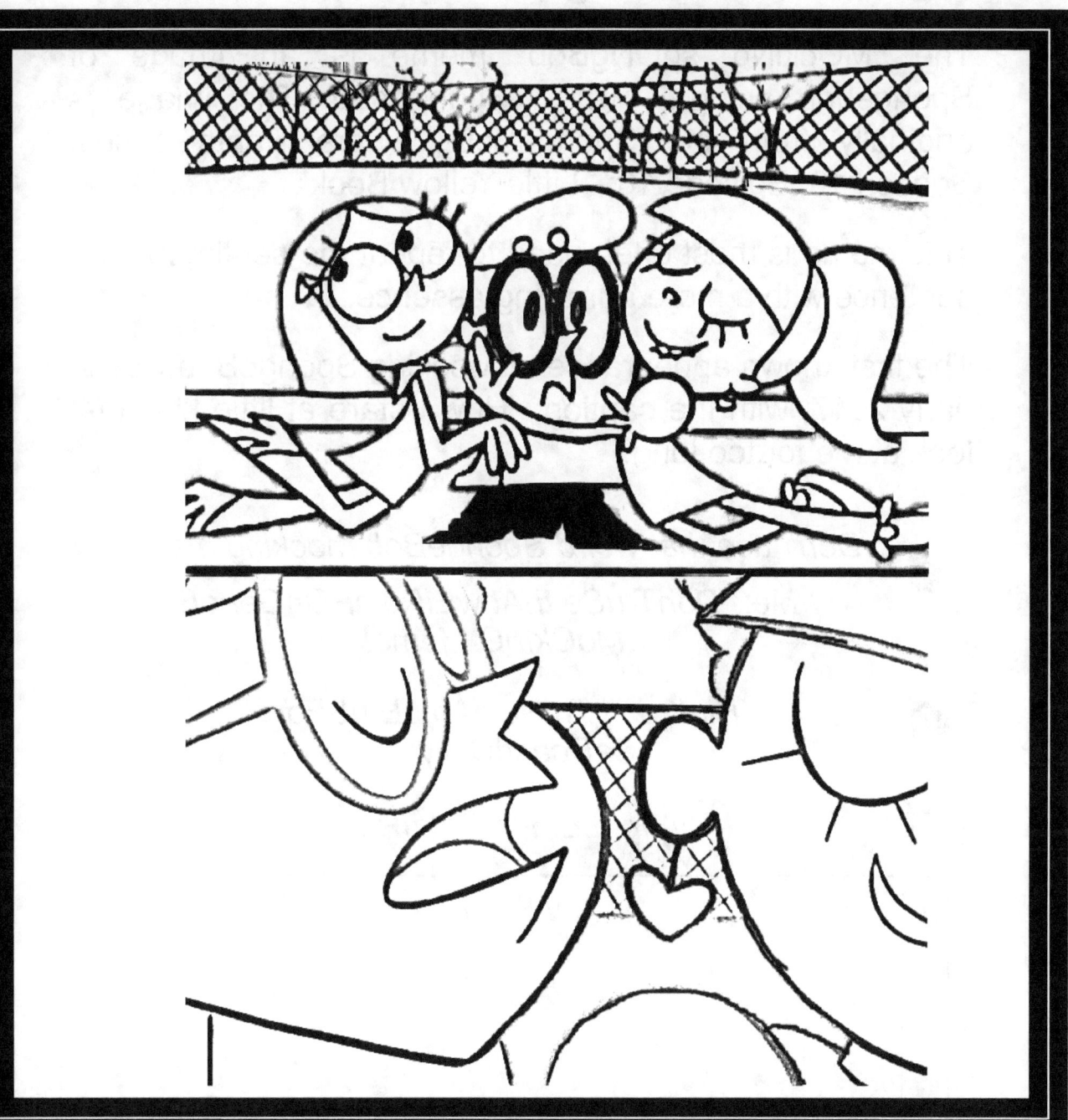

Mocking SpongeBob

The 'MOckiNg spONgBob' meme is an image of Spongebob being… well… Spongebob. The image is originally from the SpongeBob Square Pants series, Season 10, Episode 16: ' Little Yellow Book'.

This meme is most often used to repeat the sentiment of a sentence with a more annoying essence.

The first known appearance of Mocking SpongeBob was in early 2017, with the caption: "How I stare at little kids that look at me for too long."

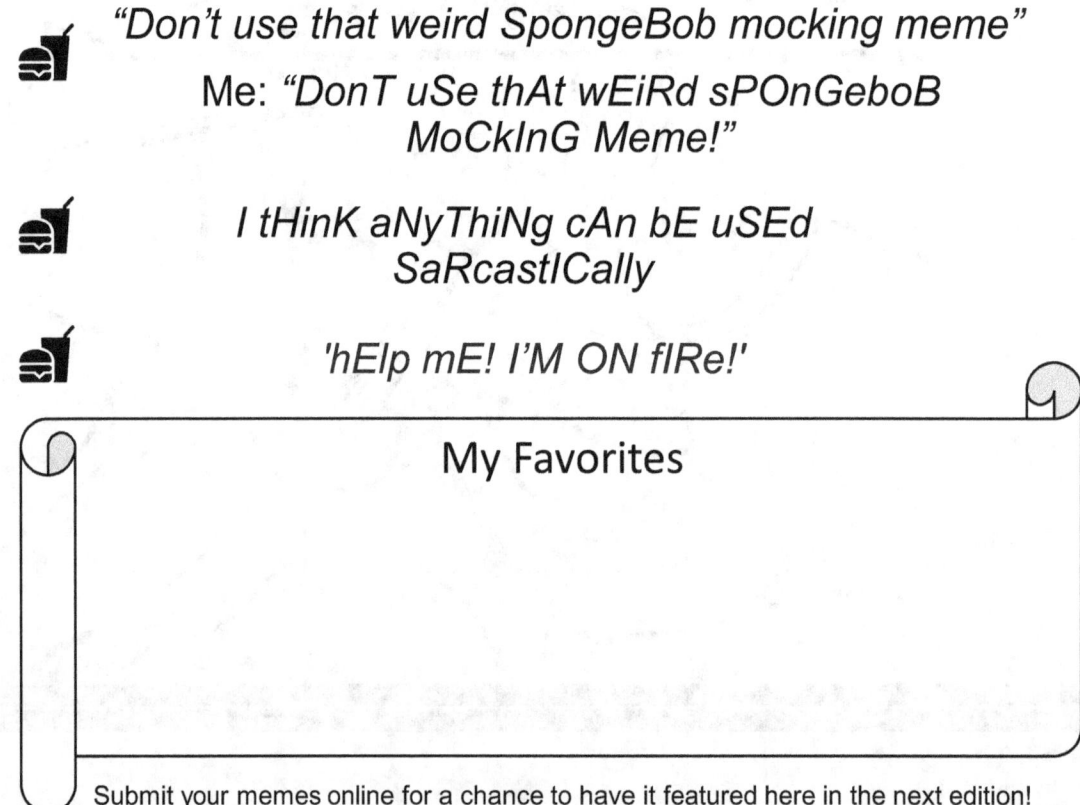

"Don't use that weird SpongeBob mocking meme"

Me: *"DonT uSe thAt wEiRd sPOnGeboB MoCkInG Meme!"*

I tHinK aNyThiNg cAn bE uSEd SaRcastICally

'hElp mE! I'M ON flRe!'

My Favorites

Submit your memes online for a chance to have it featured here in the next edition!

6

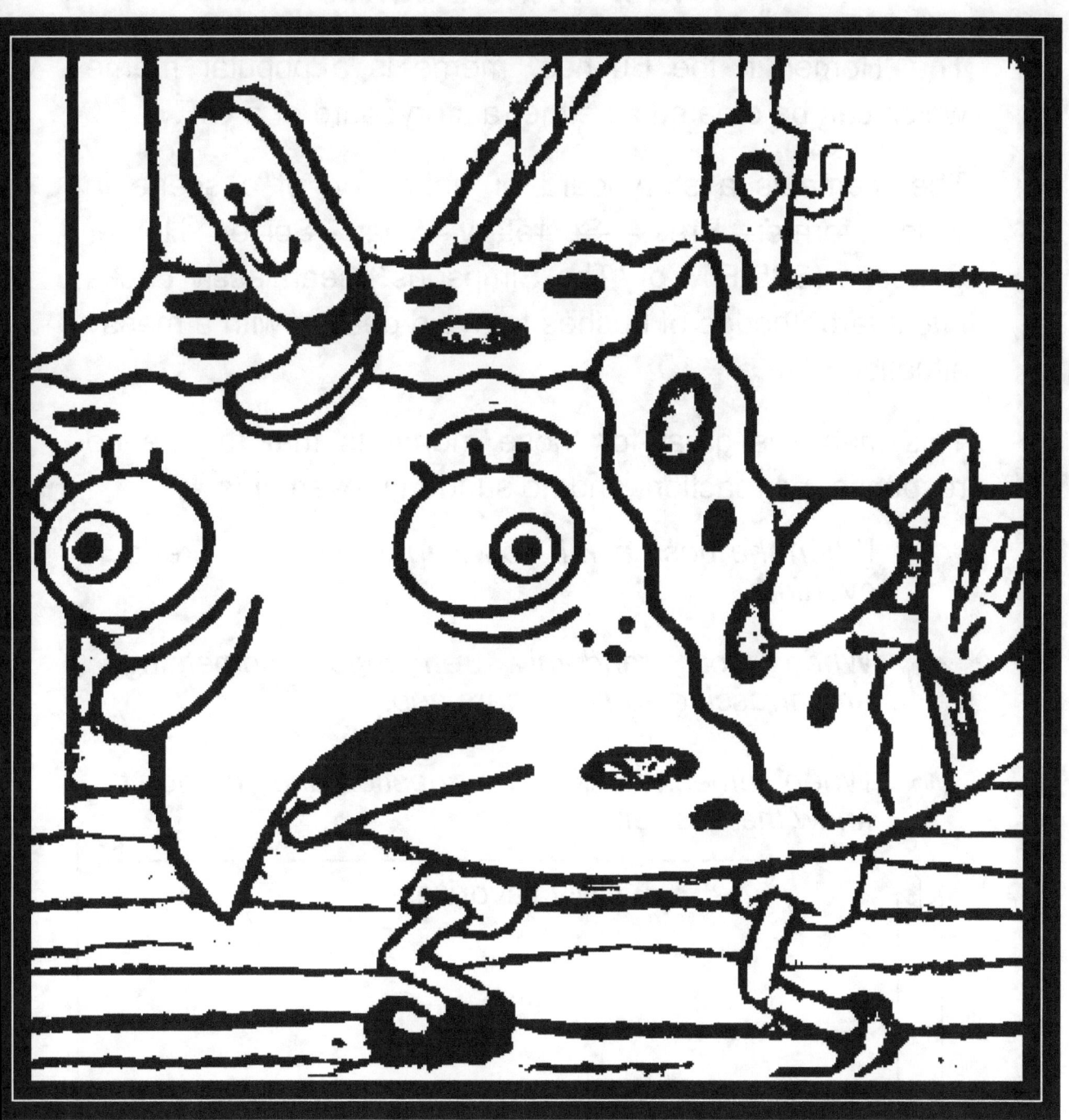

Memeology

Homer in the Bushes

The 'Homer in the Bushes" meme is a popular meme which can be created as either a storyboard or a GIF.

The meme is a storyboard or animation of a scene in which ~~former Press Secretary Sean Spicer~~ Homer Simpson (S05 E14 of "The Simpsons") seamlessly backs into a large hedge of bushes to avoid dealing with a messy situation.

This meme is great for those moments that require no response, no reaction, and no sudden movements.

- *When the boss ask if you want to work weekend overtime.*

- *When you randomly remember something embarrassing you did years ago.*

- *When someone ask you a question and you don't know the answer.*

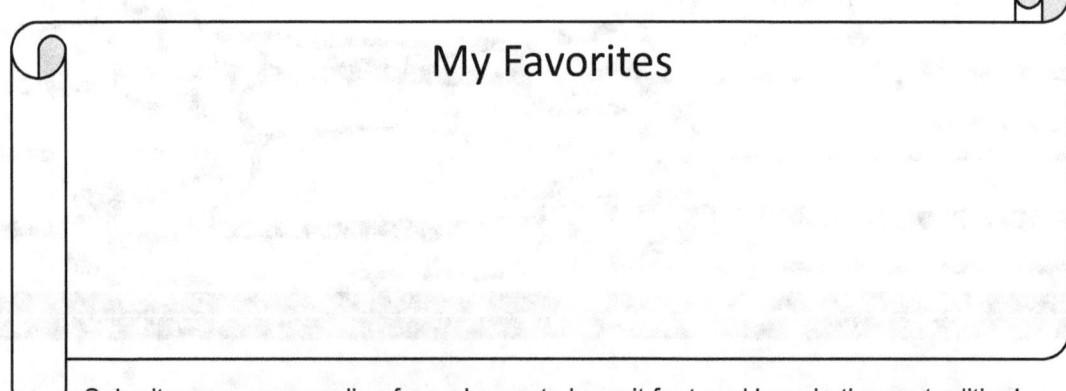

My Favorites

Submit your memes online for a chance to have it featured here in the next edition!

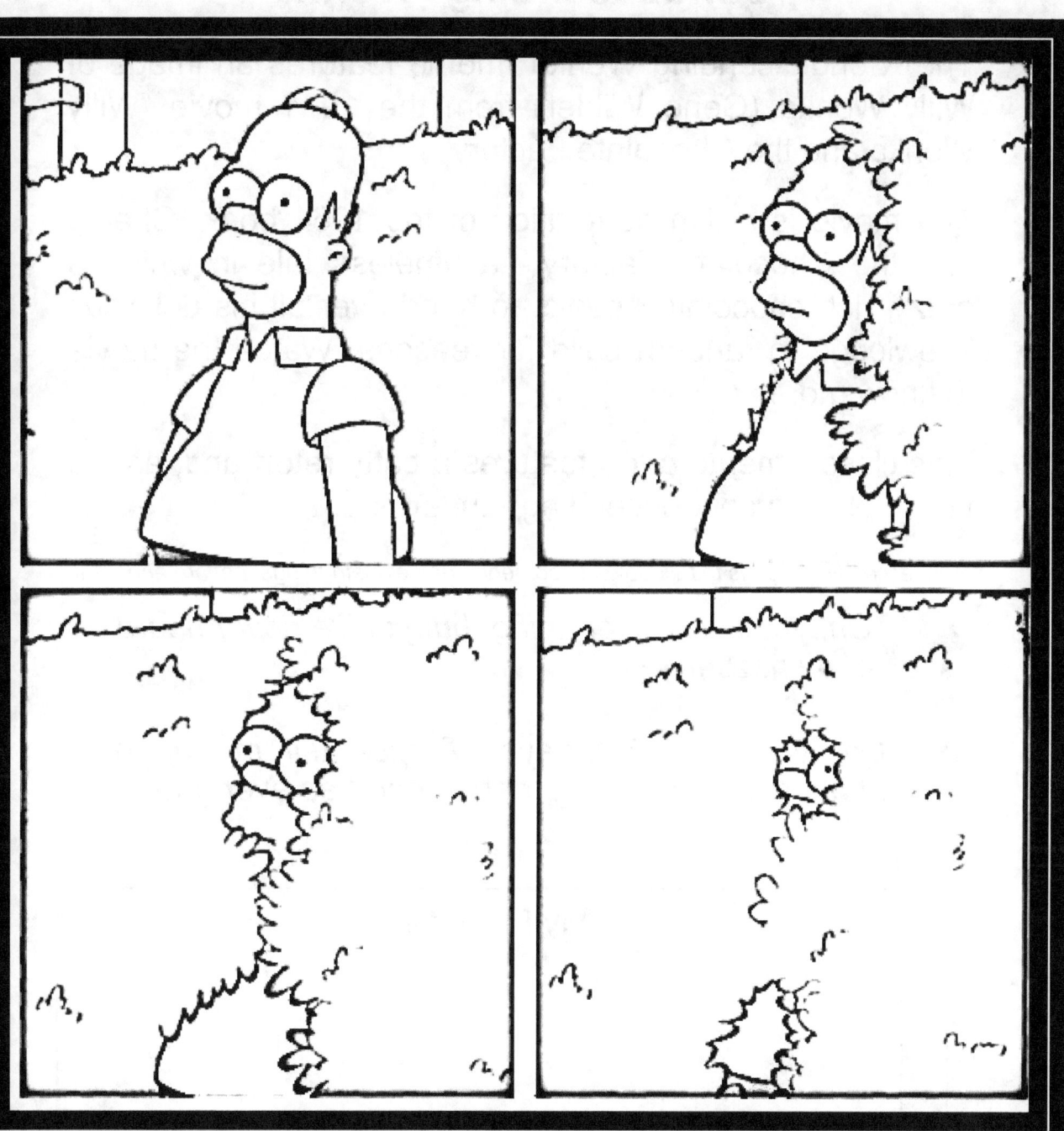

Condescending Wonka*

The "Condescending Wonka" meme features an image of Willy Wonka (Gene Wilder) from the 1971 movie "Willy Wonka and the Chocolate Factory".

The movie is a film adaptation of the 1964 book "Charlie and the Chocolate Factory"- a timeless tale in which a crazy, rich chocolatier seeks to hand over all his delicious knowledge to random child for reasons. Watch the movie to know more.

This classic meme often features a catty retort and, as the title implies, a condescending* undertone.

*condescending means to talk down to someone and explain things that are apparent

 Oh, you know everything, but you've never heard of a snozberry?

 Oh, you hate Mondays? Please tell me more about this new feeling that no one has ever had.

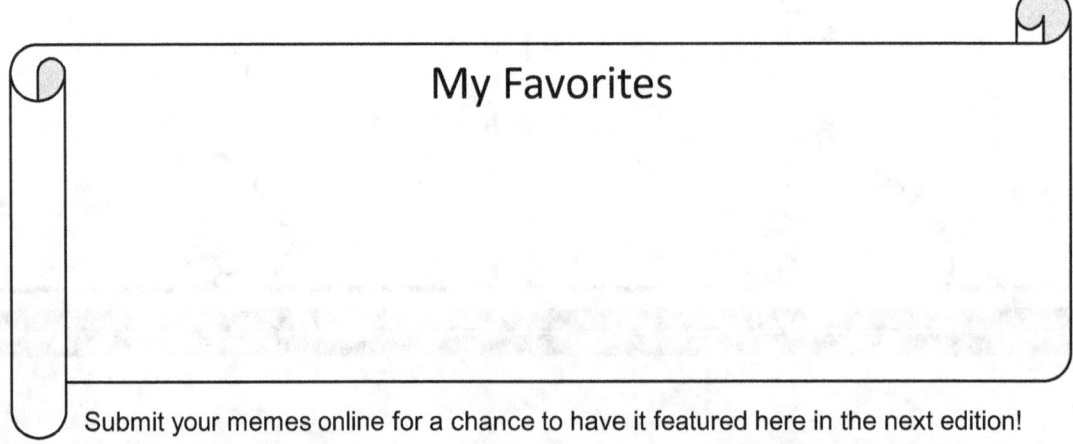

My Favorites

Submit your memes online for a chance to have it featured here in the next edition!

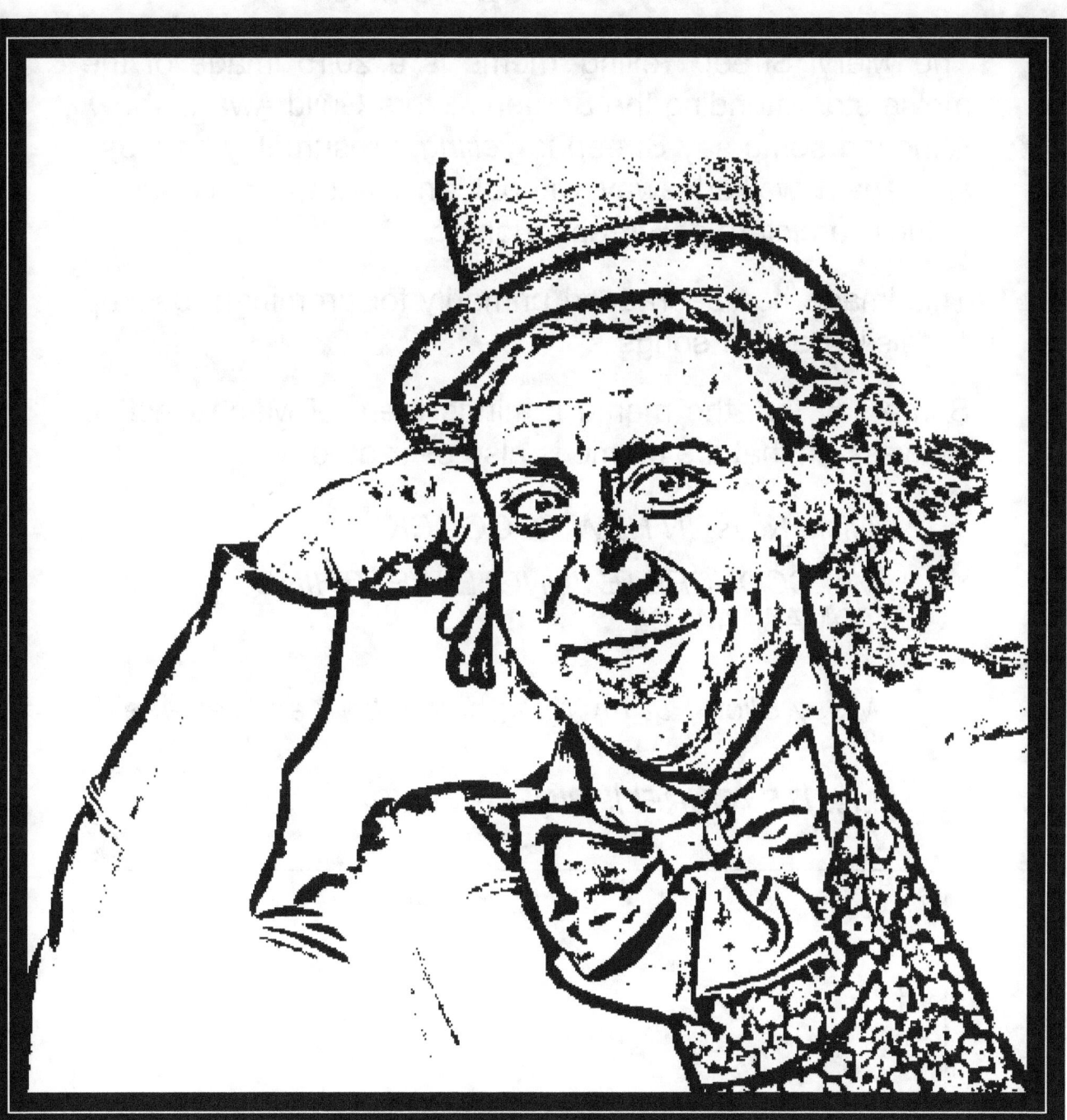

Memeology

Meryl Streep Yelling

The 'Meryl Streep Yelling' meme is a 2015 image of the movie star attending the Screen Actors Guild Award show. Although some say Streep is *yelling,* presumably because she again walked away without an award, the image is actually a picture of Streep laughing.

This image has been used primarily for prominent backup vocals in popular songs.

Some say that the meme reminds them of Meryl's acting prowess- in that the meme is also overrated.

Alicia Keys: IN NEW YOOOORK

Me: CCONCRETE JUNGLE WET THING TOMAAAAATO!!

Missy Eliot: Put my thing down flip it and reverse it

Me: ITSYOURFLIPPINFLENYET!!

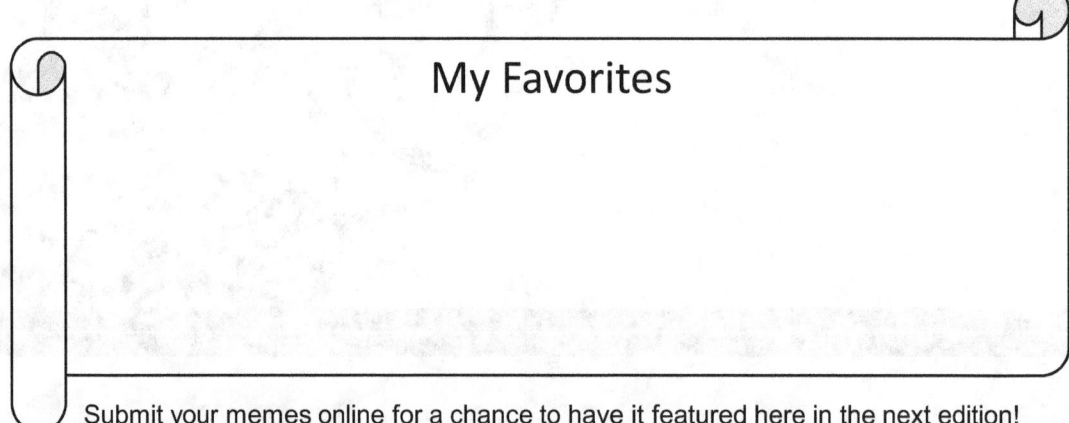

My Favorites

Submit your memes online for a chance to have it featured here in the next edition!

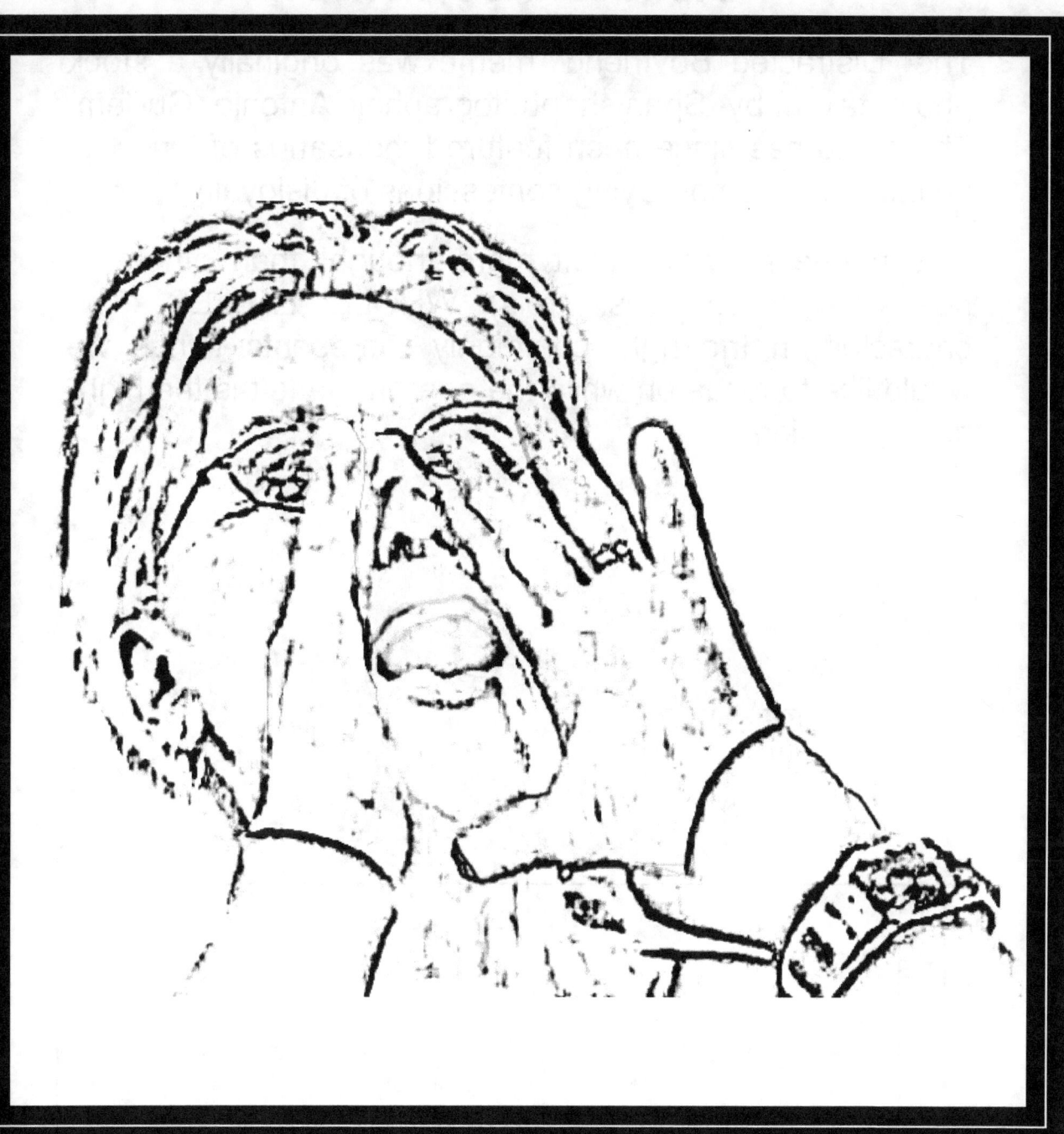

Distracted Boyfriend

The "Distracted Boyfriend" meme was originally a stock photo taken by Spanish photographer Antonio Guillem. The photo has since been featured thousands of times as an internet joke portraying confessions of disloyalty.

This meme requires a bit more thought than others. It needs 3 (three, tres, trois) WHOLE LABLES. The character on the right commonly represents things we would like to focus on while the one on the left is the high-risk distraction.

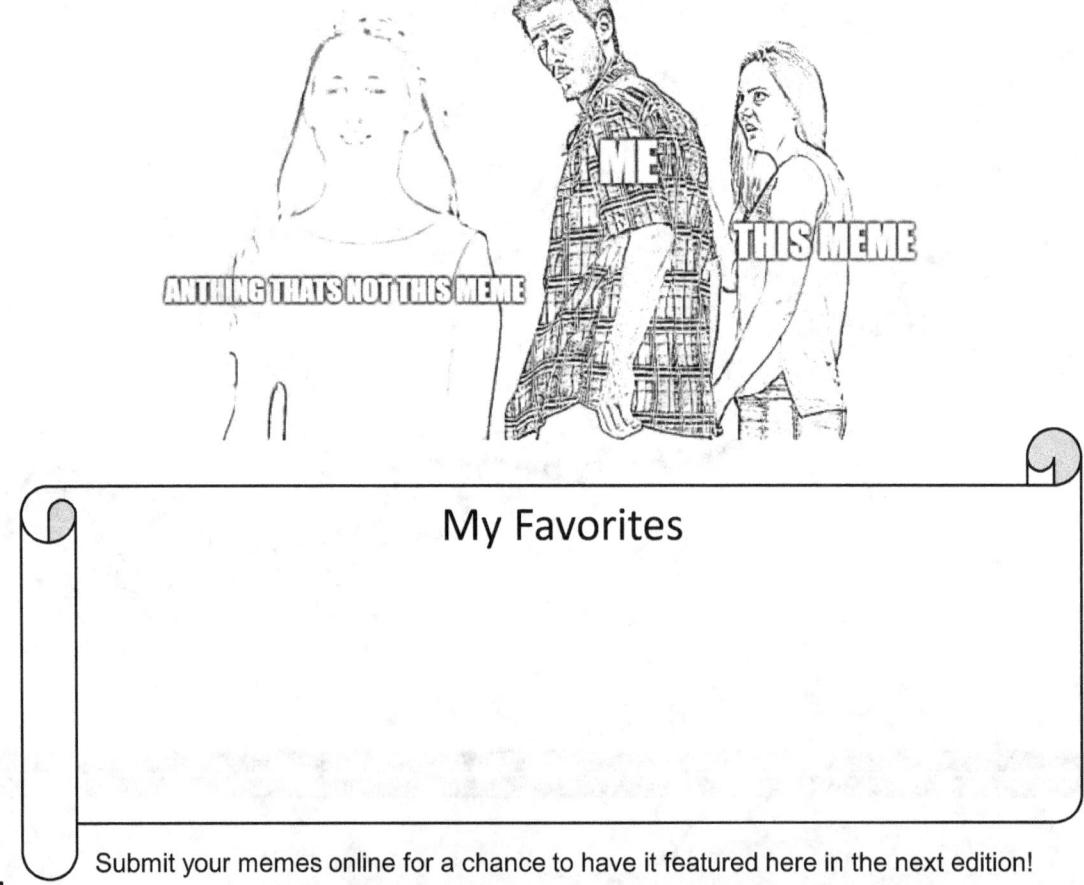

My Favorites

Submit your memes online for a chance to have it featured here in the next edition!

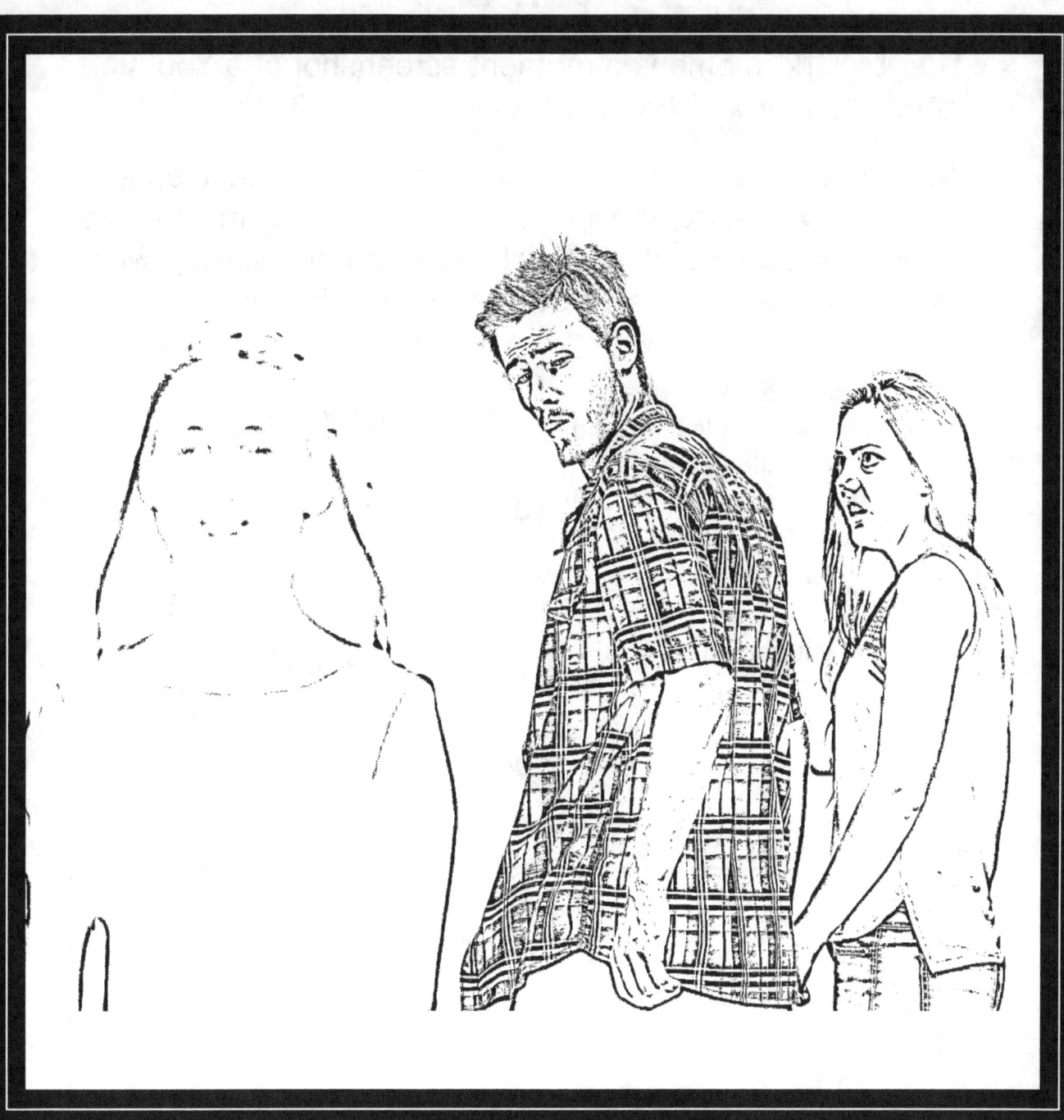

Exit 12

The "Exit 12" meme is a moment screenshot of a YouTube video titled 'How to Exit the Freeway Like a Boss'.

When used, the offramp sign is filled with two choices and the car swerves to the preferred option. The meme has commonly been used to depict instances of following what your heart really wants as well as fair-weather fandom.

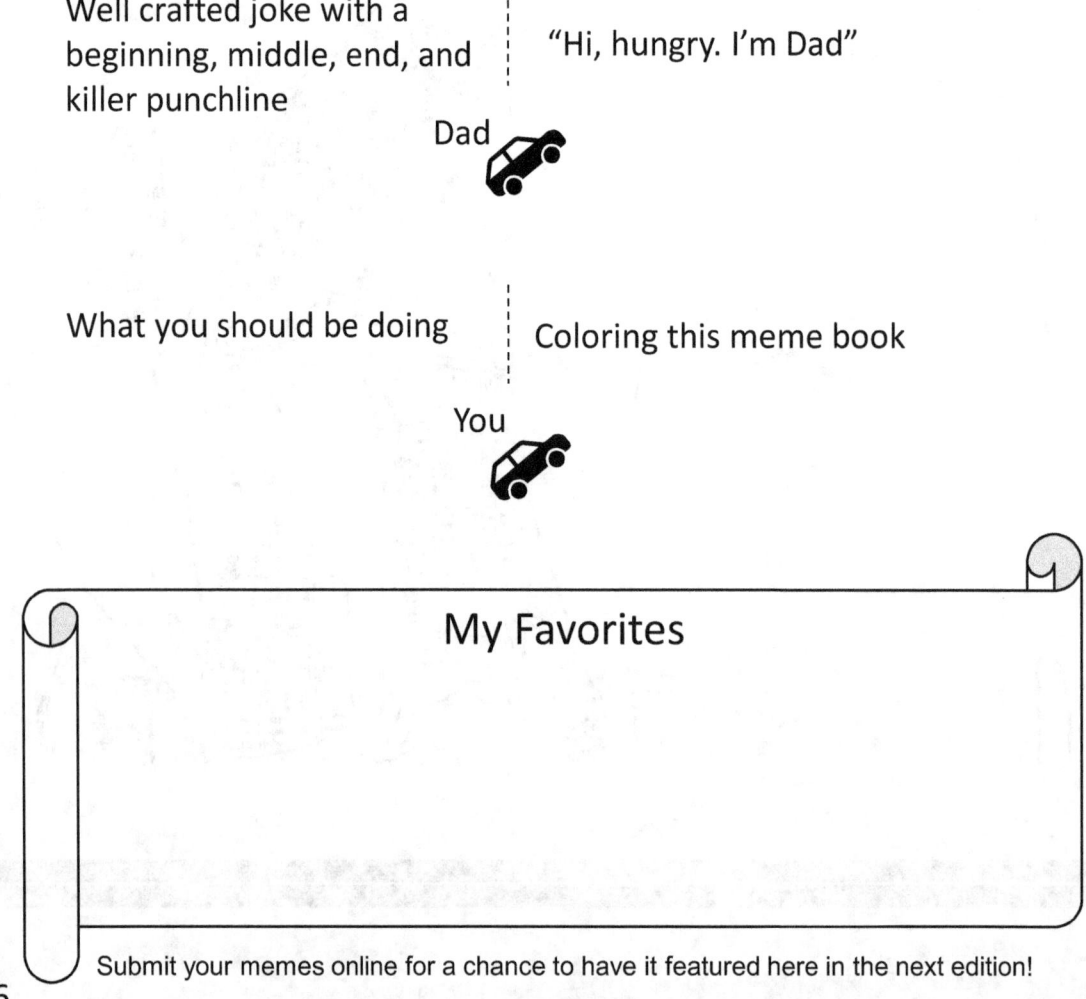

Well crafted joke with a beginning, middle, end, and killer punchline

"Hi, hungry. I'm Dad"

Dad

What you should be doing

Coloring this meme book

You

My Favorites

Submit your memes online for a chance to have it featured here in the next edition!

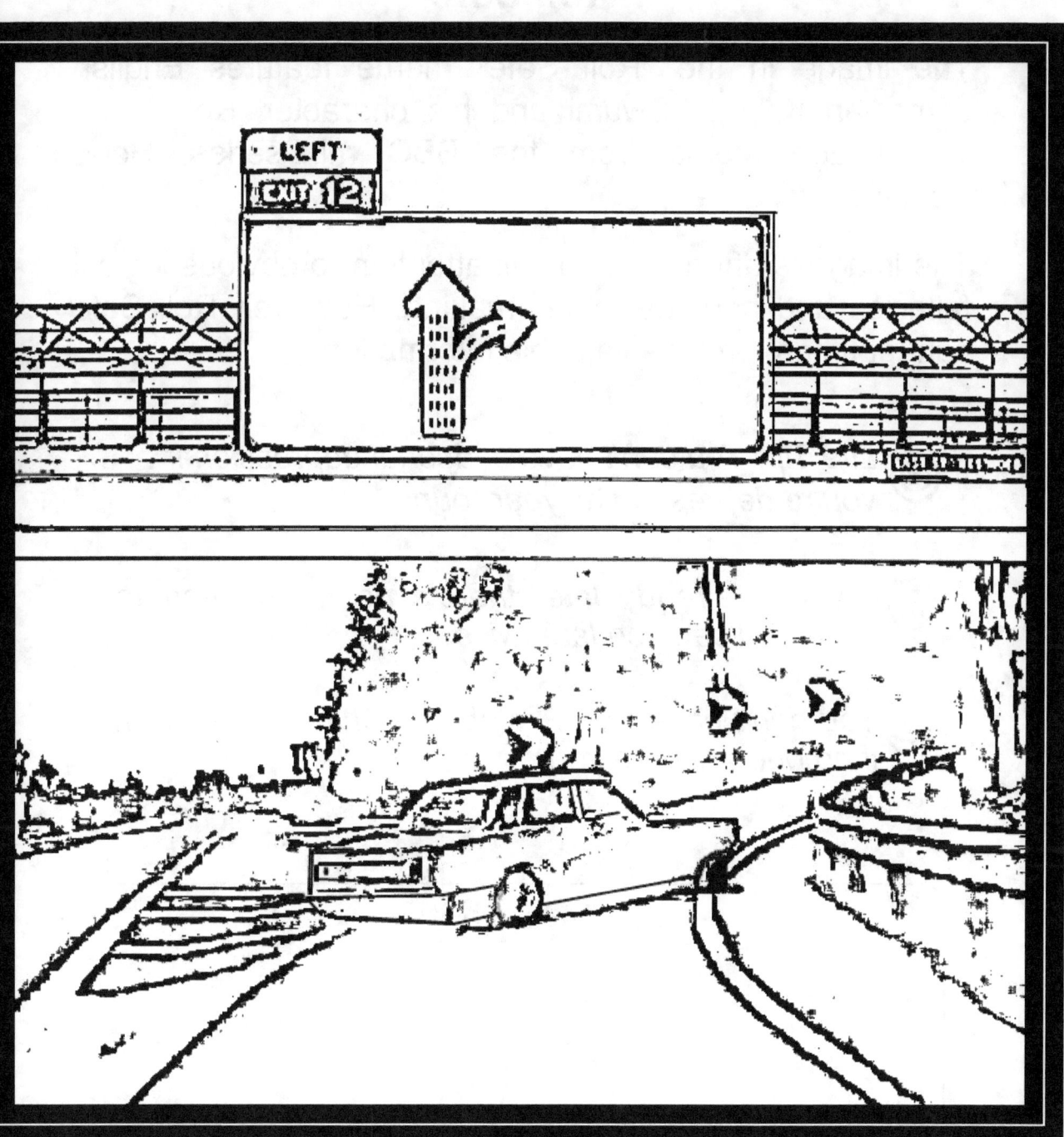

Memeology

Roll Safe

The image in the "Roll Safe" meme features English comedian Kayode Ewumi and his character 'Roll Safe'. The image stems from the BBC mini-series 'Hood Documentary'.

The image is often used to call attention to obvious logical fallacies and poor decision making. However, Roll Safe can (at times) provide valuable information.

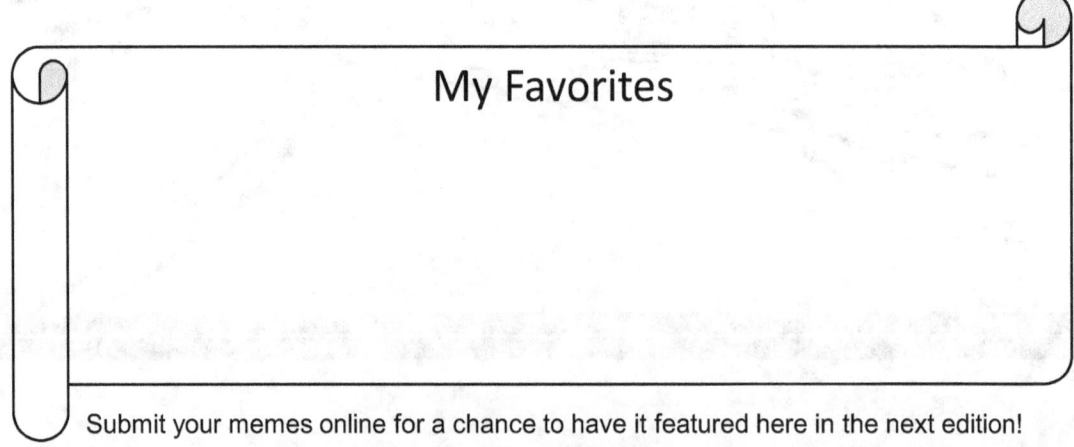

Life Tip: You can't have seasonal depression if you're depressed all year round.

If you're already late, there's no more need to rush. You can't be late twice…..

You don't have to worry about getting cheated on if no one will date you.

My Favorites

Submit your memes online for a chance to have it featured here in the next edition!

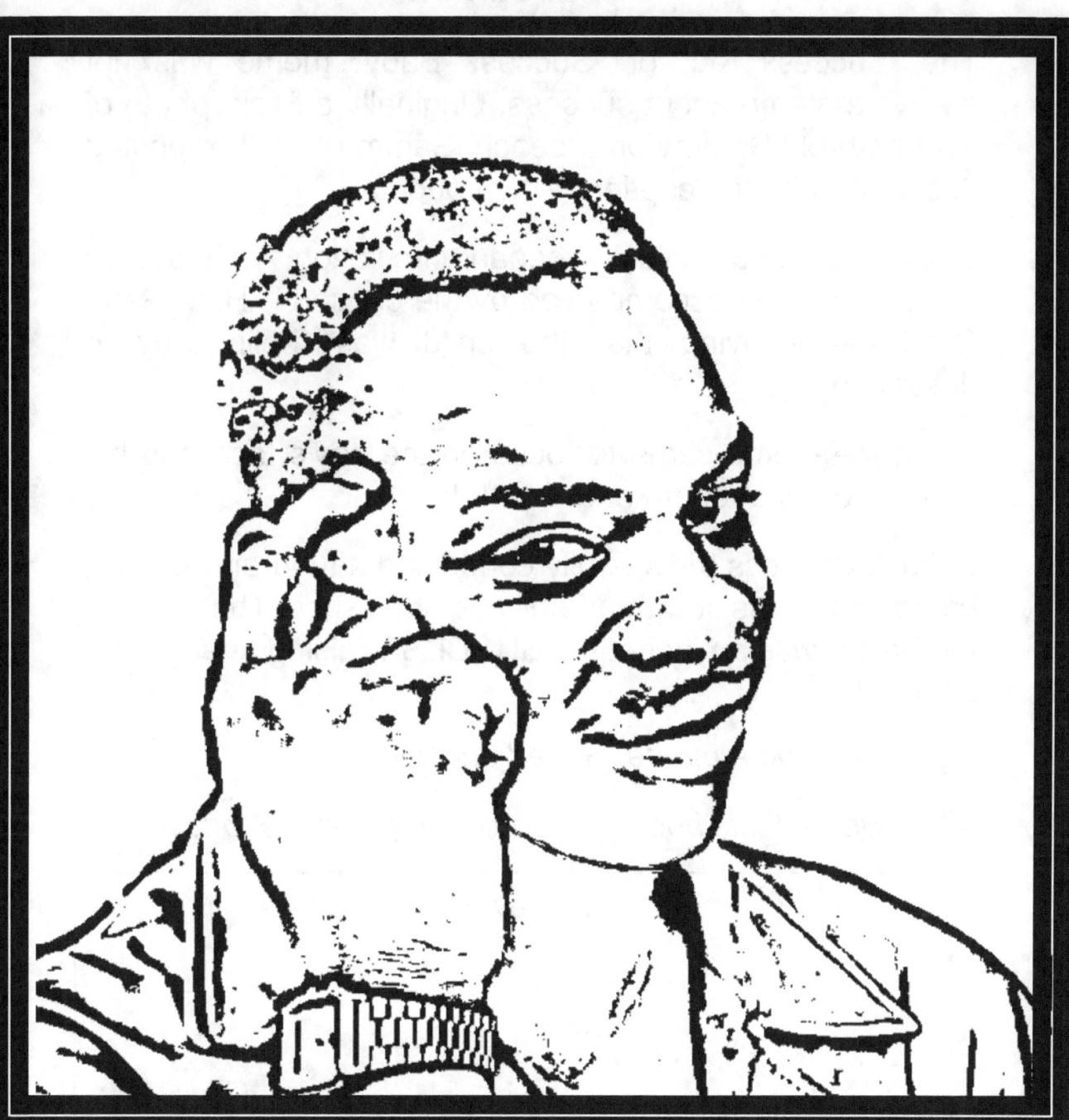

M e m e o l o g y

Success Kid

The "Success Kid" or "Success Baby" meme was not always a meme about success. Originally a Flickr photo of 11-month-old Sammy on a beach, Sammy's mother posted this photo with the caption "Why I oughta…"

Since the image initially began circulation, it has also commonly been accompanied by the caption "I Hate Sand Castles"-- implying that the child was feeling joy in destruction.

Later, the meme came to focus on the boy's face and his expression of strength and fortitude.

In 2015 Success Kid's family conducted a fundraising campaign to assist with a family health issues. The fundraiser was an incredible SUCCESS raising nearly $100,000!

 Became a meme. Saved dad's life!

 Bought this book. Did something creative today!

My Favorites

Submit your memes online for a chance to have it featured here in the next edition!

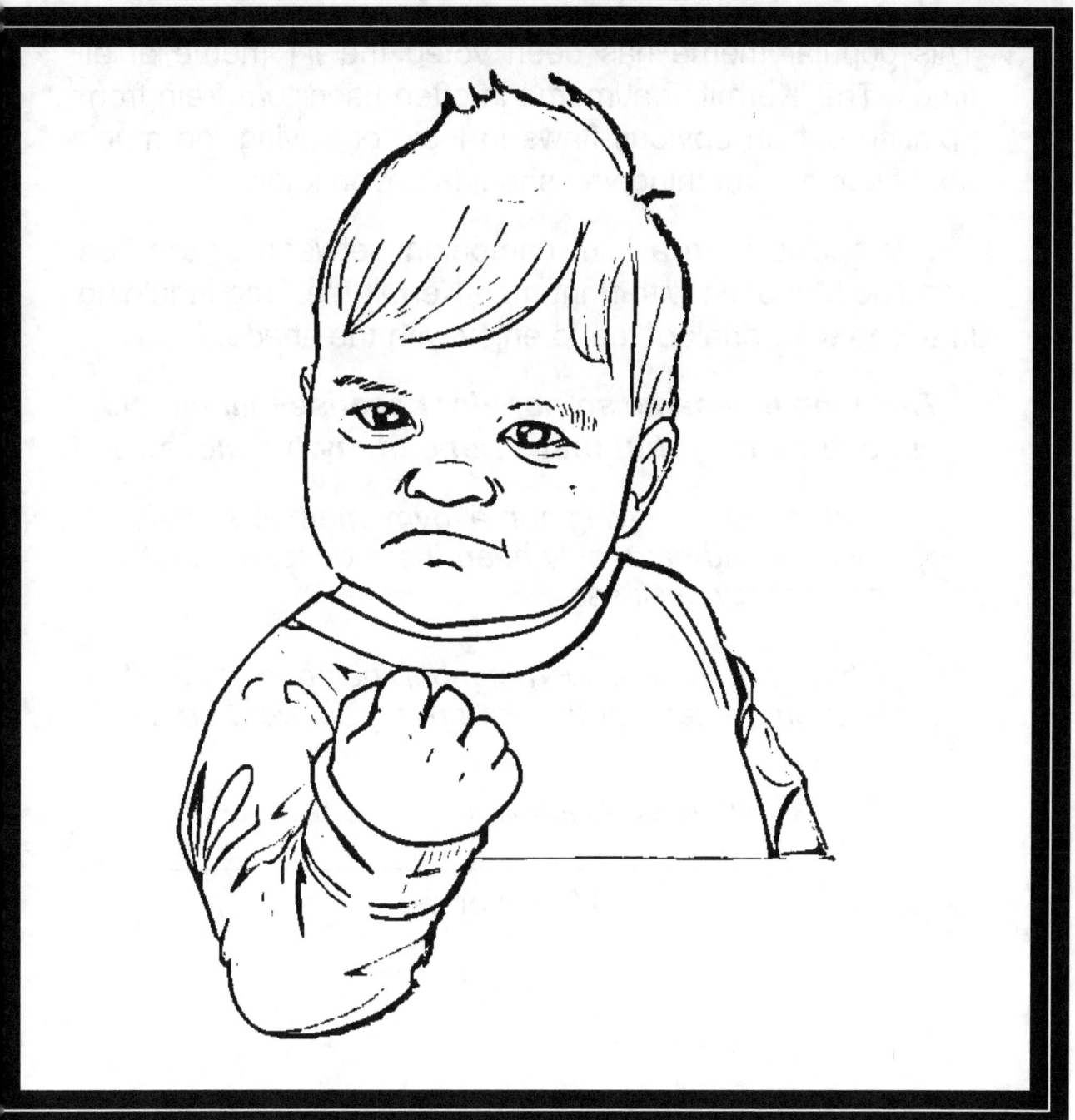

Kermit Tea

This popular meme has been voted the #1 meme of all times. The 'Kermit Tea' meme is often used to refrain from pointing out an obvious flaws in logic or saying too much about some something you shouldn't even know.

The image is from a joint campaign between Lipton Tea and The Muppets, with front man Kermit the Frog indulging in a long slow drink of tea to enjoy with the shade.

This meme became so popular because millennials are extra shady; but that's none of my business....

 You've been paying for a gym membership for months and have only been there once, but that's none of my business…

 When you hear your neighbor being robbed at 3am but remember that he put a password on his Wi-Fi.

So that's none of my business.

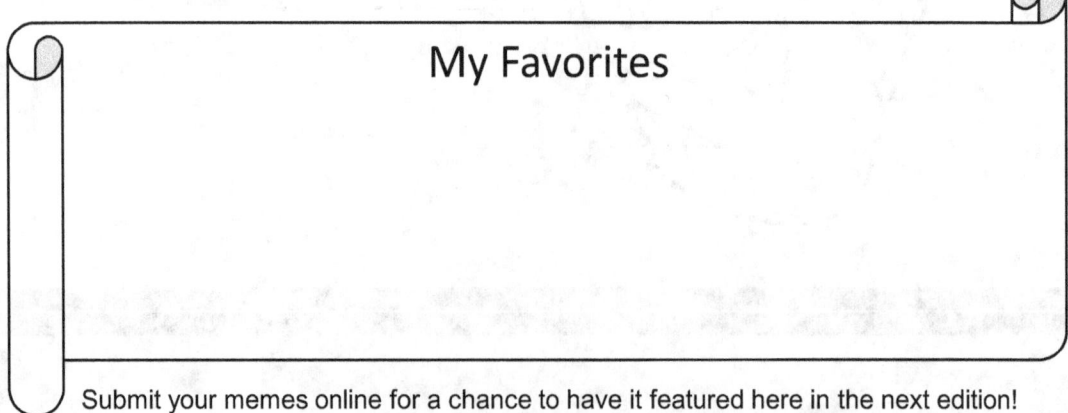

My Favorites

Submit your memes online for a chance to have it featured here in the next edition!

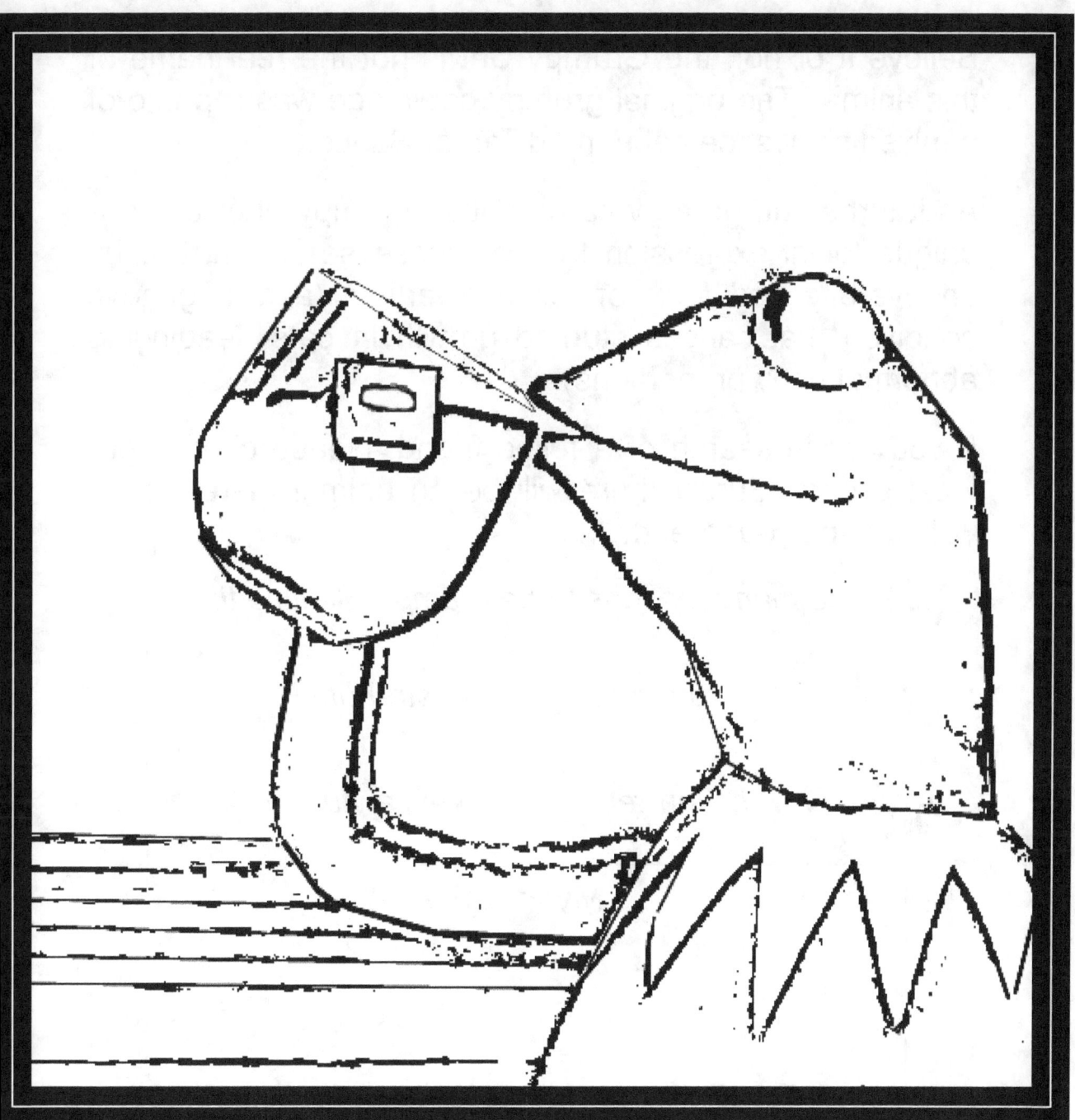

M e m e o l o g y

Grumpy Cat

Believe it or not, the Grumpy Cat is not the real name of this animal. The original grumpy cat image was a photo of a mixed snowshoe cat named Tardar Sauce.

As it turns out, grumpy cat is not so grumpy after all. The unique facial expression the cat possesses is caused by an overbite and form of feline dwarfism (a rare genetic condition that causes stunted growth in cats- leading to abnormal body proportions).

If you are in search of a feline friend, please check your local shelter. Surely there will be an animal there that is willing to be your friend….

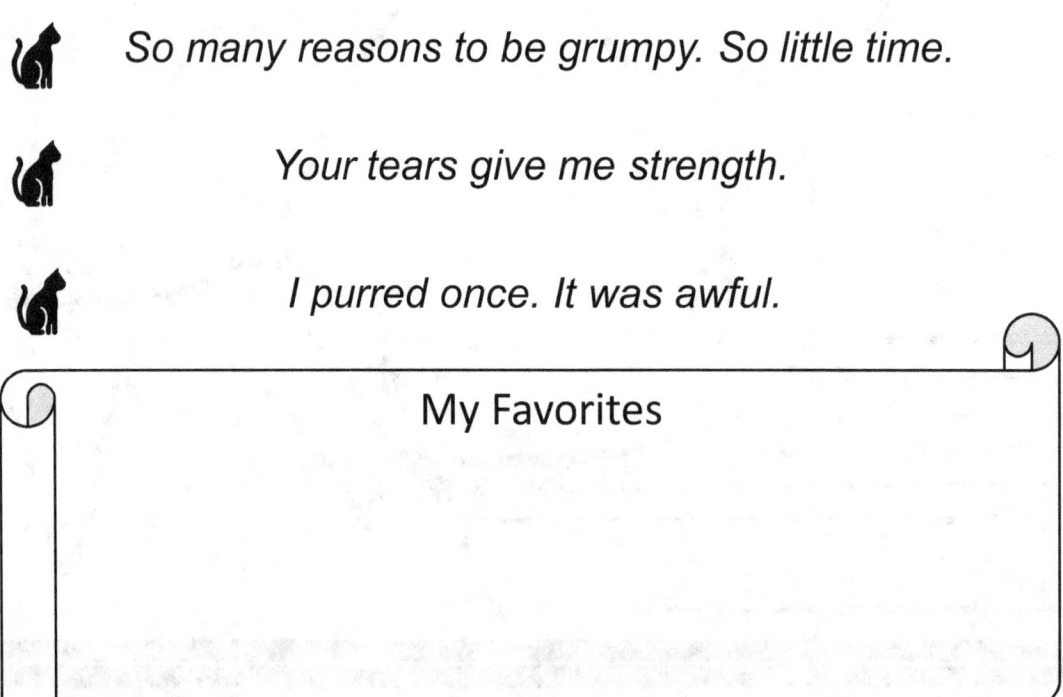

So many reasons to be grumpy. So little time.

Your tears give me strength.

I purred once. It was awful.

My Favorites

Submit your memes online for a chance to have it featured here in the next edition!

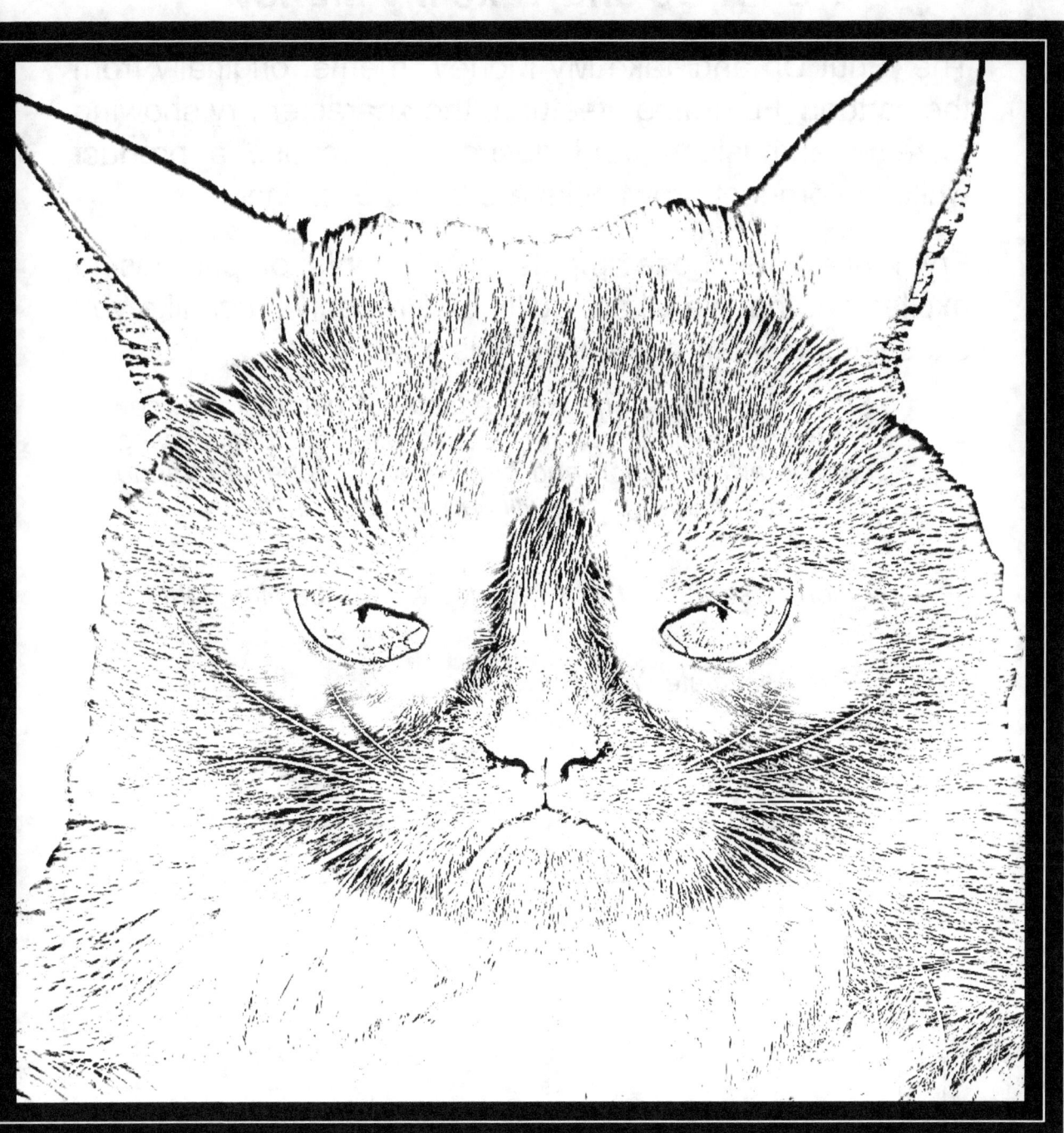

Shut Up and Take My Money

The "Shut Up and Take My Money" meme, originally from the cartoon 'Futurama', features the character Fry showing extreme enthusiasm and desire to purchase a product while the product drawbacks are being explained.

Fry represents those impulsive moments of purchasing excitement that we all are guilty of. Probably much like you experienced when purchasing this book.

Store Associate: The side effects of carrying the new Iphone 27 include: death, loss of life, no longer living, cardiac arrest, vision and hearing loss, appetite change, and your neighbors' dog will bark at you constantly.

 Iphone Users: But the messages will still be blue right?

Store Associate: Yes, But…..

Iphone Users:

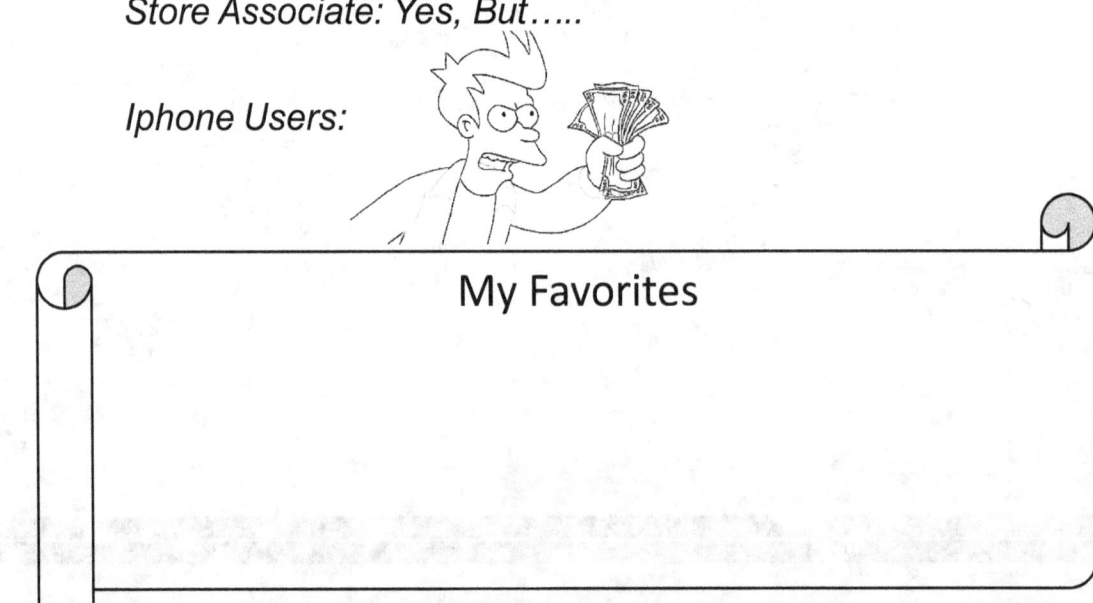

My Favorites

Submit your memes online for a chance to have it featured here in the next edition!

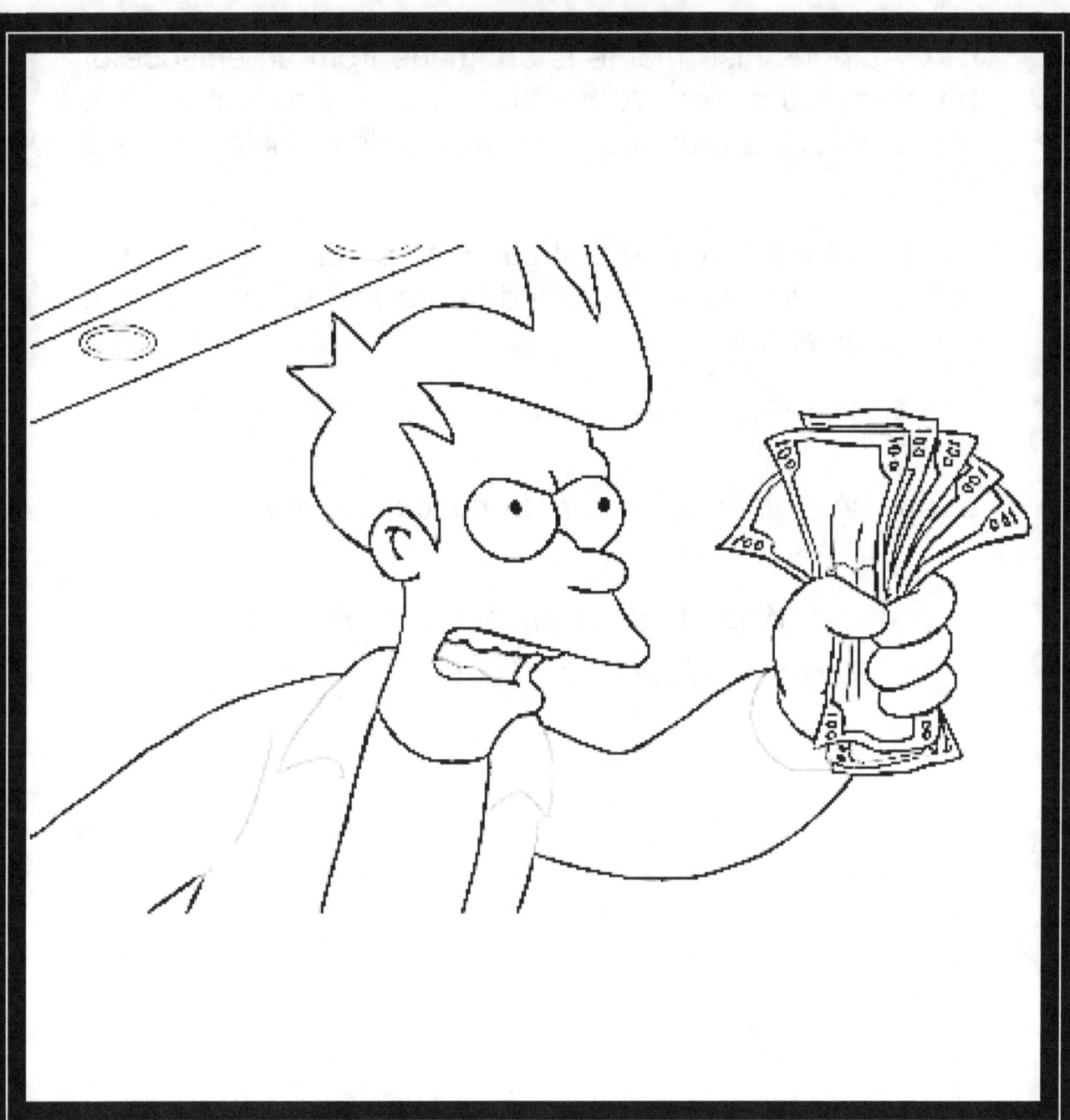

Arthur's Fist

The "Author's Fist" meme is an image from an episode of the animated series "Arthur" in which the title character, Arthur, must learn to deal with moments of instantaneous anger.

This is not the first time that characters from the animated series 'Arthur' has been turned into a meme, but it is the most popular time.

😠 *When someone says memes aren't funny*

😠 *When they tell you that the ice cream machine is down.*

😠 Me: *"What do you want to do for dinner tonight?"*

Person: *"I don't care."*

Me:

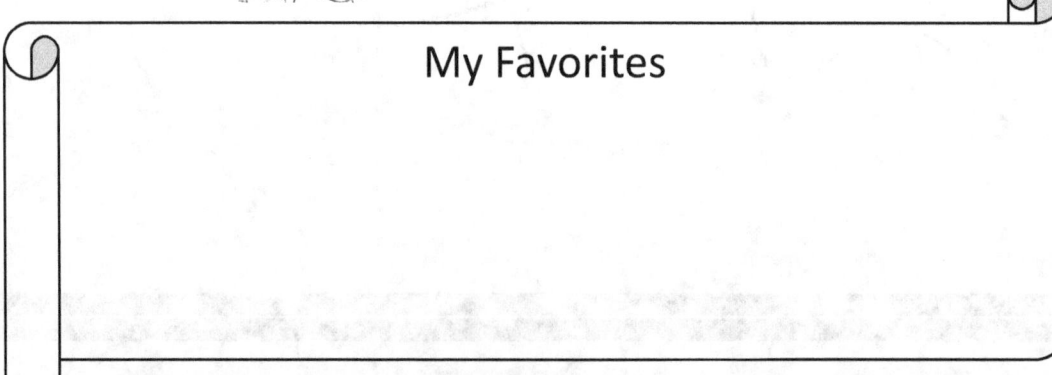

My Favorites

Submit your memes online for a chance to have it featured here in the next edition!

28

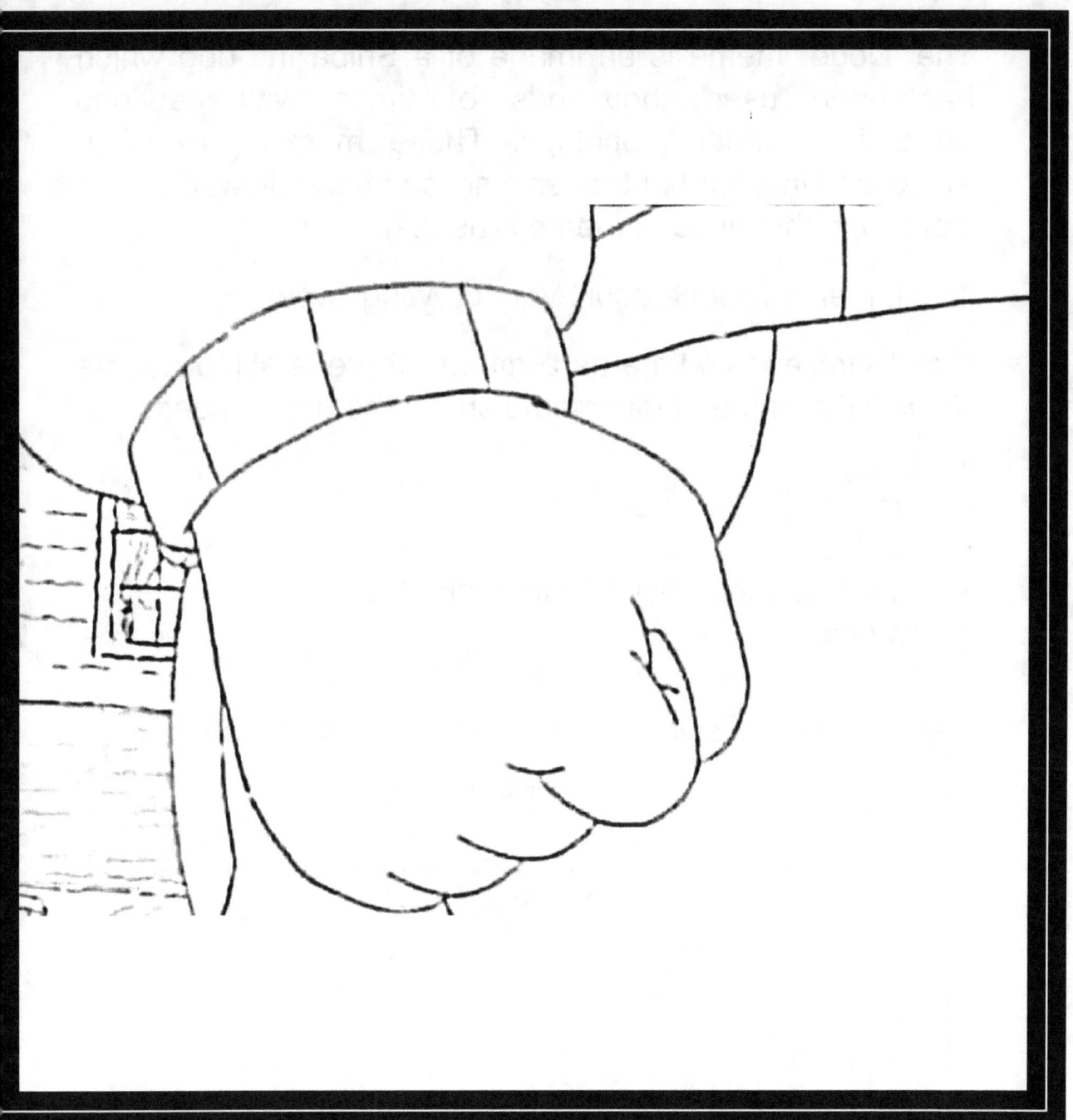

Doge

The "Doge" meme is an image of a Shiba Inu dog which has been used thousands of times with captions describing inner monologs. These memes are often expressed in a kind of broken English often followed by the word wow (because of meme reasons).

'Much memes' 'Such book' Very drawing' 'wow'

Even after all this time as a meme, there is still a debate on how the name of this meme should be pronounced.

- *Doggy*
- *Doge*
- *Dodge*
- *Any other sounds you can think of…..*
- *wow*

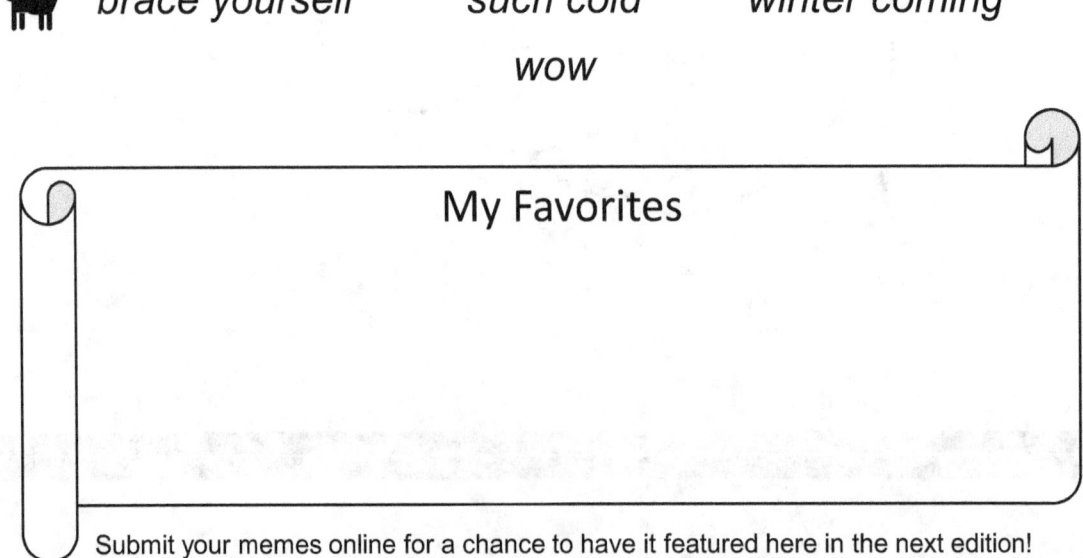 *brace yourself*   *such cold*   *winter coming*

wow

My Favorites

Submit your memes online for a chance to have it featured here in the next edition!

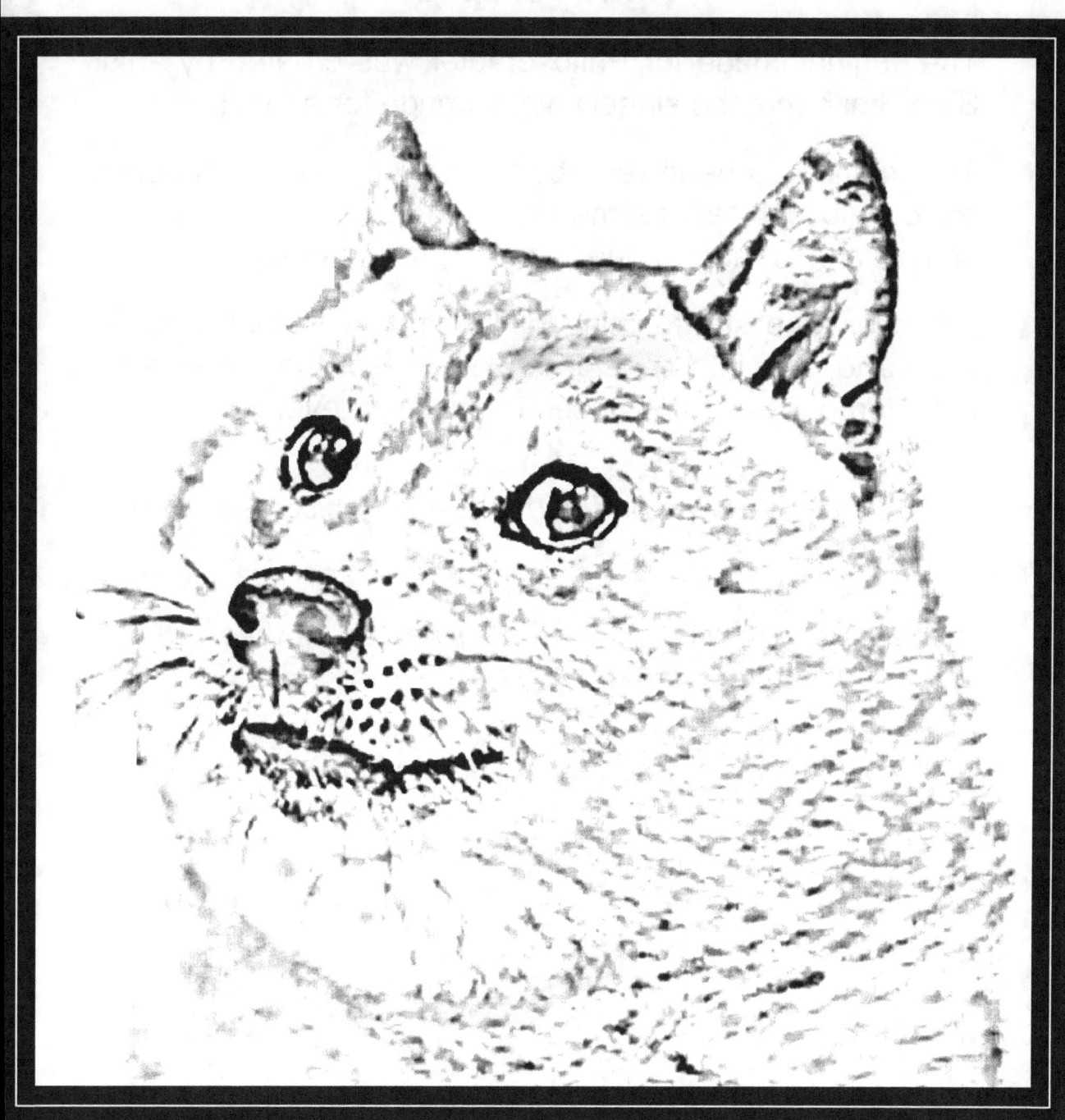

Memeology

Philosoraptor

The original image for Philosoraptor was created by artist Sam Smith (not the singer) as an image for a t-shirt.

The meme has been reproduced on the internet to depict deep philosophical arguments (often using flawed logic) to convince the reader of the argument's legitimacy.

However, one shortcoming of the meme is that it never seems to take into consideration the fact that no one on the internet can be convinced of anything, ever.

If you try to fail and you succeed, which have you done?

Does expecting the unexpected make the unexpected the expected?

Why is abbreviation such a long word?

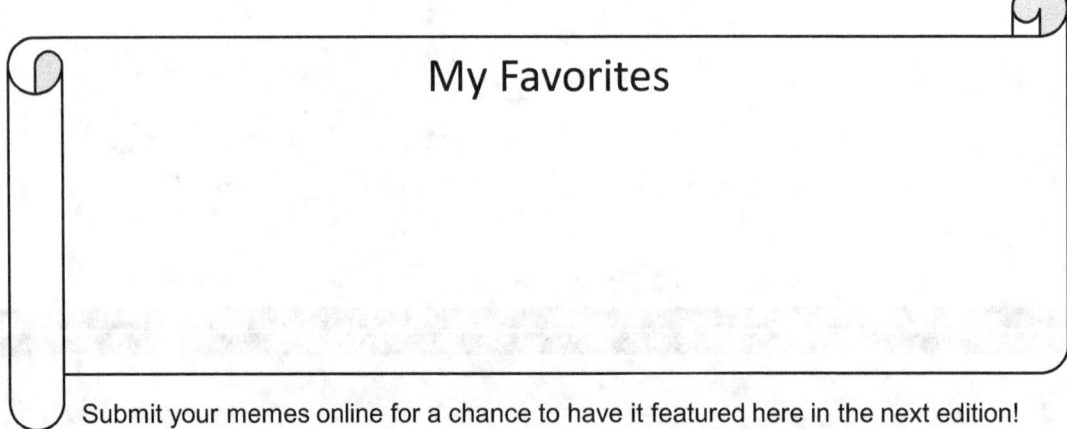

My Favorites

Submit your memes online for a chance to have it featured here in the next edition!

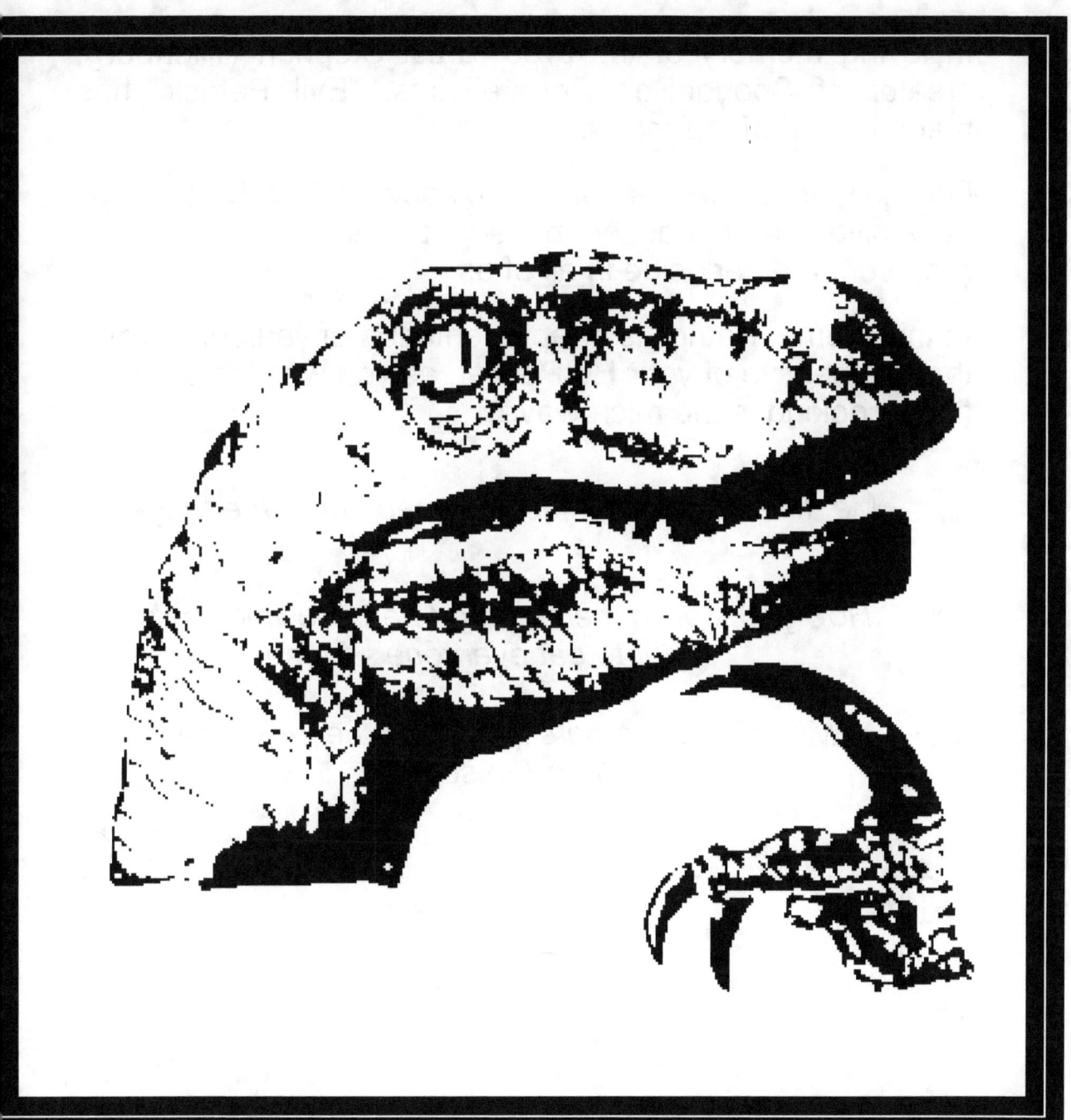

Memeology

Evil Patrick

In loving memory of the great artist Stephen Hillenburg, creator of SpongeBob SquarePants, "Evil Patrick" has made the list of top memes.

Originally from the Season 1, Episode 'Nature Pants' This pervasive meme has been used thousands of times to represent the dark side in all of us.

In this meme, Patrick is a representation of yourself—from the perspective of your HotPocket, as you wait for it to finish cooking in the microwave.

☛ *Me, kicking the ice I just dropped under the fridge.*

☛ *How you look in the fast food bag knowing you're about to eat everyone's fries.*

☛ *Me leaving the pots in the sink because they 'need to soak'.*

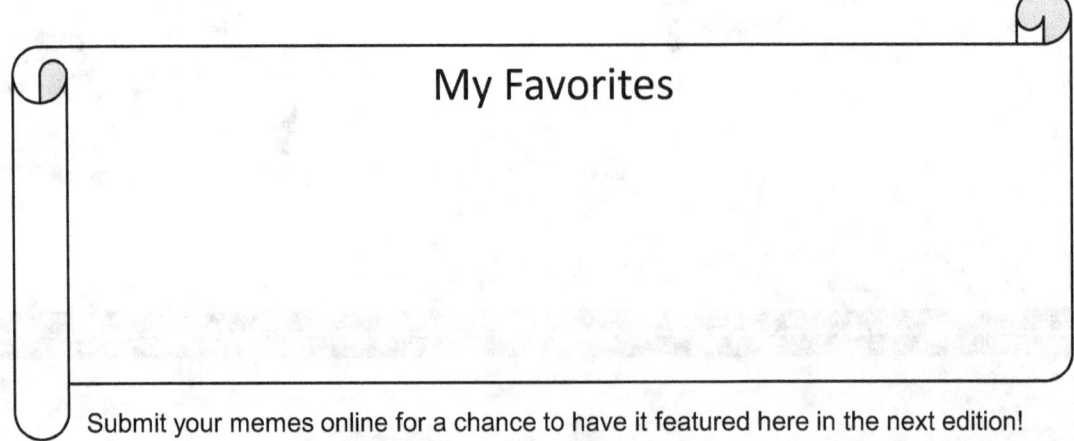

My Favorites

Submit your memes online for a chance to have it featured here in the next edition!

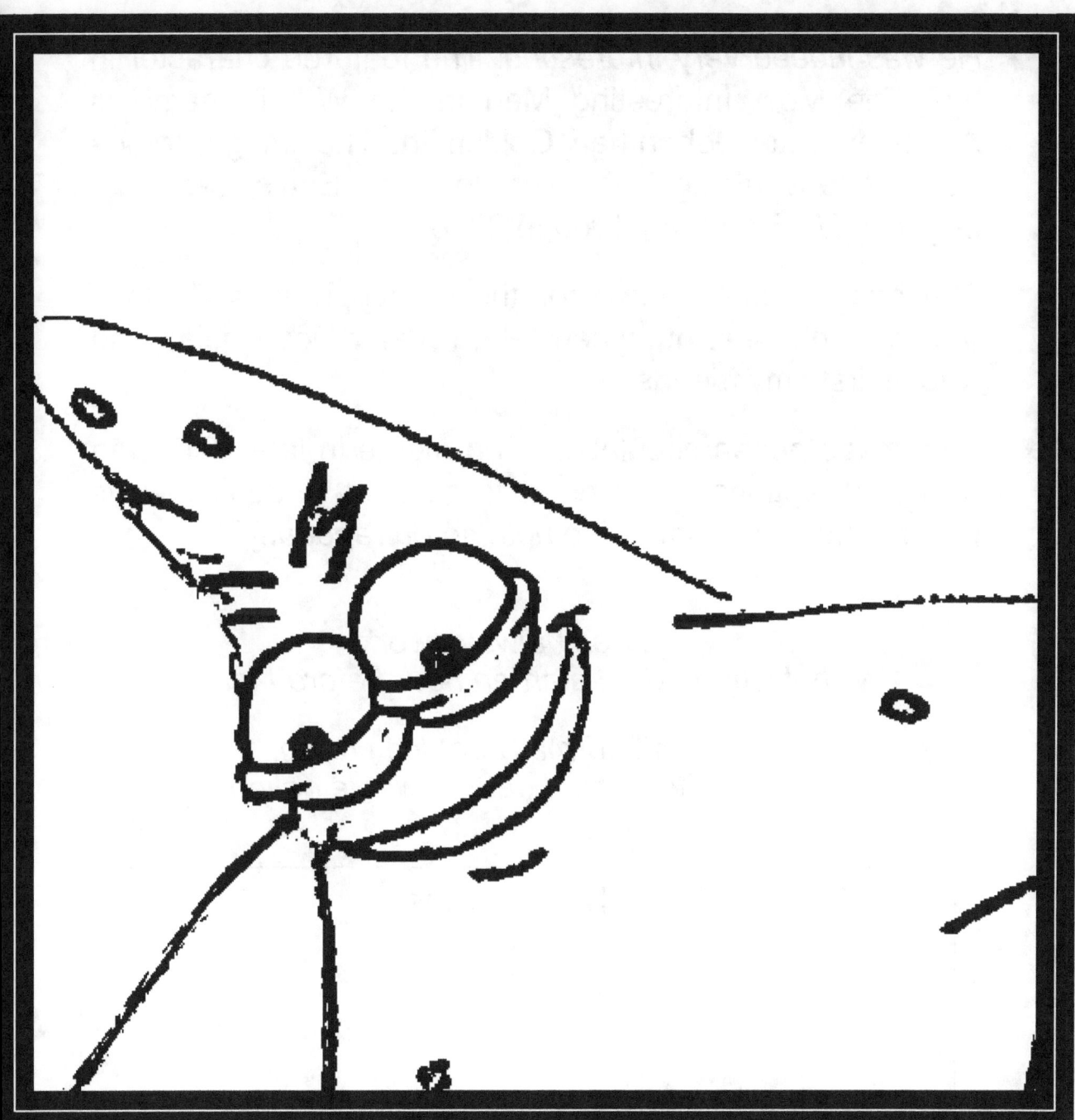

Memeology

The Most Interesting Man in the World

He was indeed very interesting. The featured character in the "The Most Interesting Man in the World" meme is American actor Johnathan Goldsmith. The image comes from an advertising campaign for Dos Equis beer that began in 2006 and ran through 2018.

The ads became known for their catchphrases, "I don't always drink beer, but when I do, I prefer Dos Equis." and "Stay thirsty my friends."

The image began circulation as a meme in late 2017 with hilarious captions following a formula of "I don't always [*action*], but when I do, I [*something outrageous*]."

I don't always work,
but when I do, I start an hour before I leave.

I don't normally eat ice cream,
but when I do, I eat the whole gallon.

My Favorites

Submit your memes online for a chance to have it featured here in the next edition!

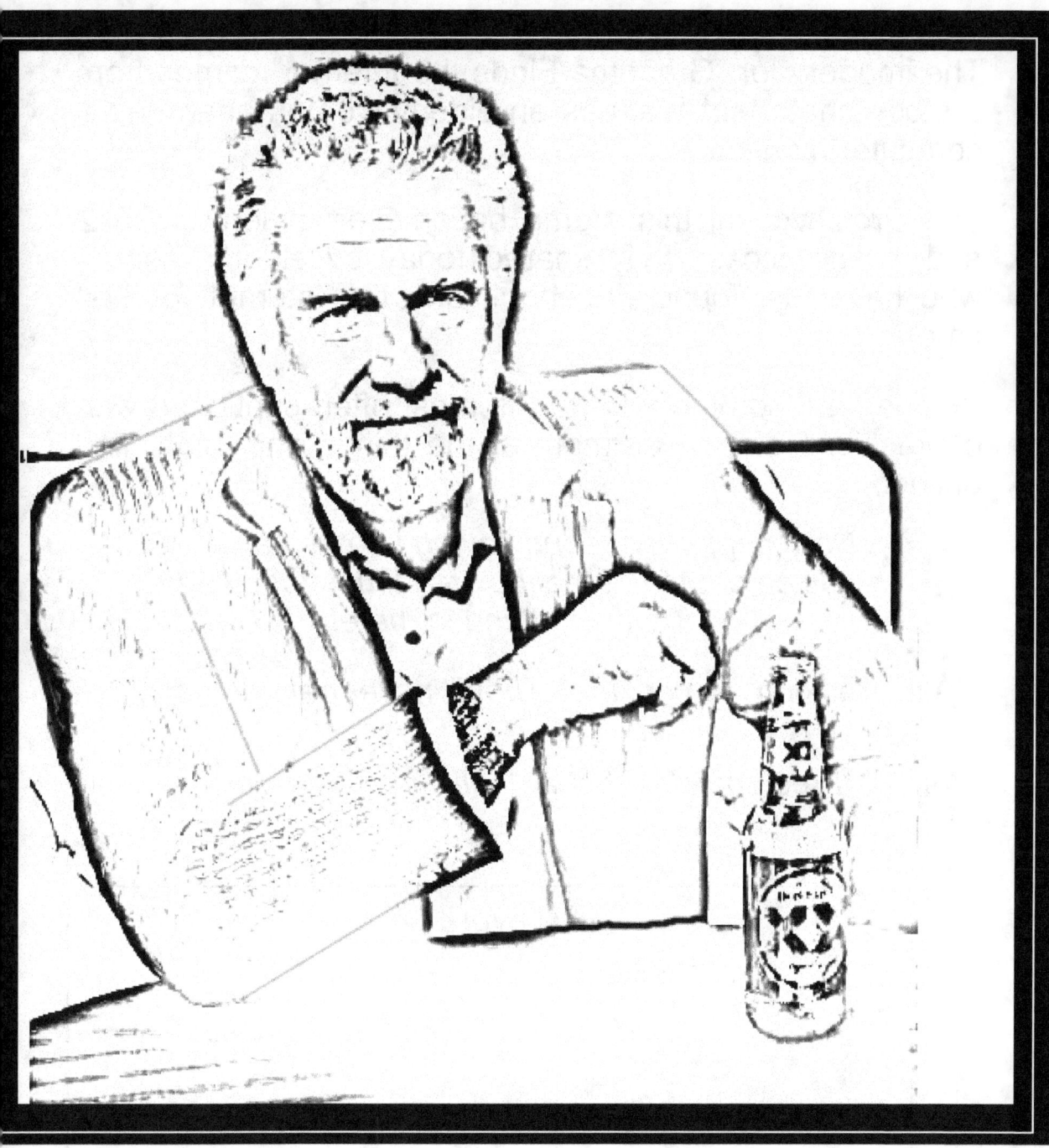

Memeology

Grandma Finds the Internet

The imagery for "Grandma Finds the Internet" comes from a stock photo that features an elderly woman analyzing a computer monitor.

The circulation of this meme became prominent in 2012 and is still occasionally shared today by elderly woman who have just found Facebook and the internet for first time.

"Grandma Finds the Internet" is most often captioned with expressions of bewilderment at the things one might find online.

 Darn computer keeps saying I have mail. I've walked out to the mailbox ten times today and there's nothing in there!

 Tracking my cookies? They'll never get my recipe!

 Free spam? What a deal! Spam is delicious!

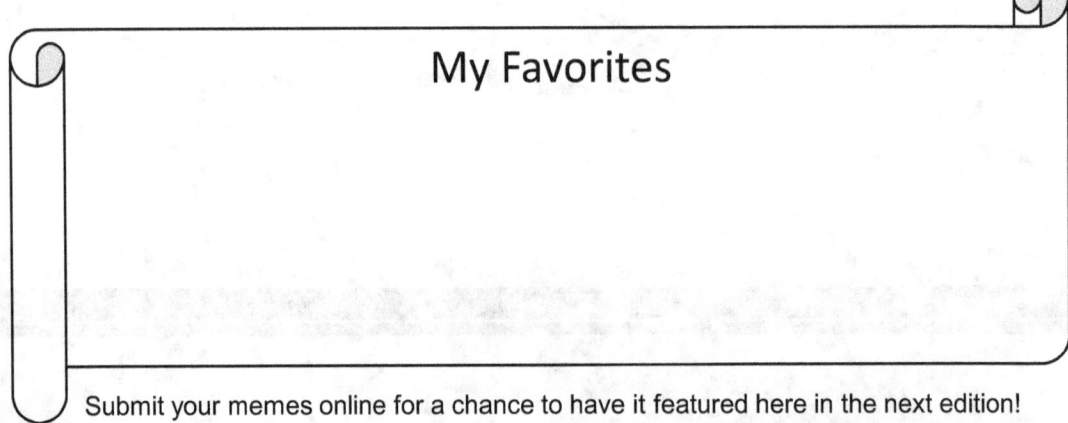

My Favorites

Submit your memes online for a chance to have it featured here in the next edition!

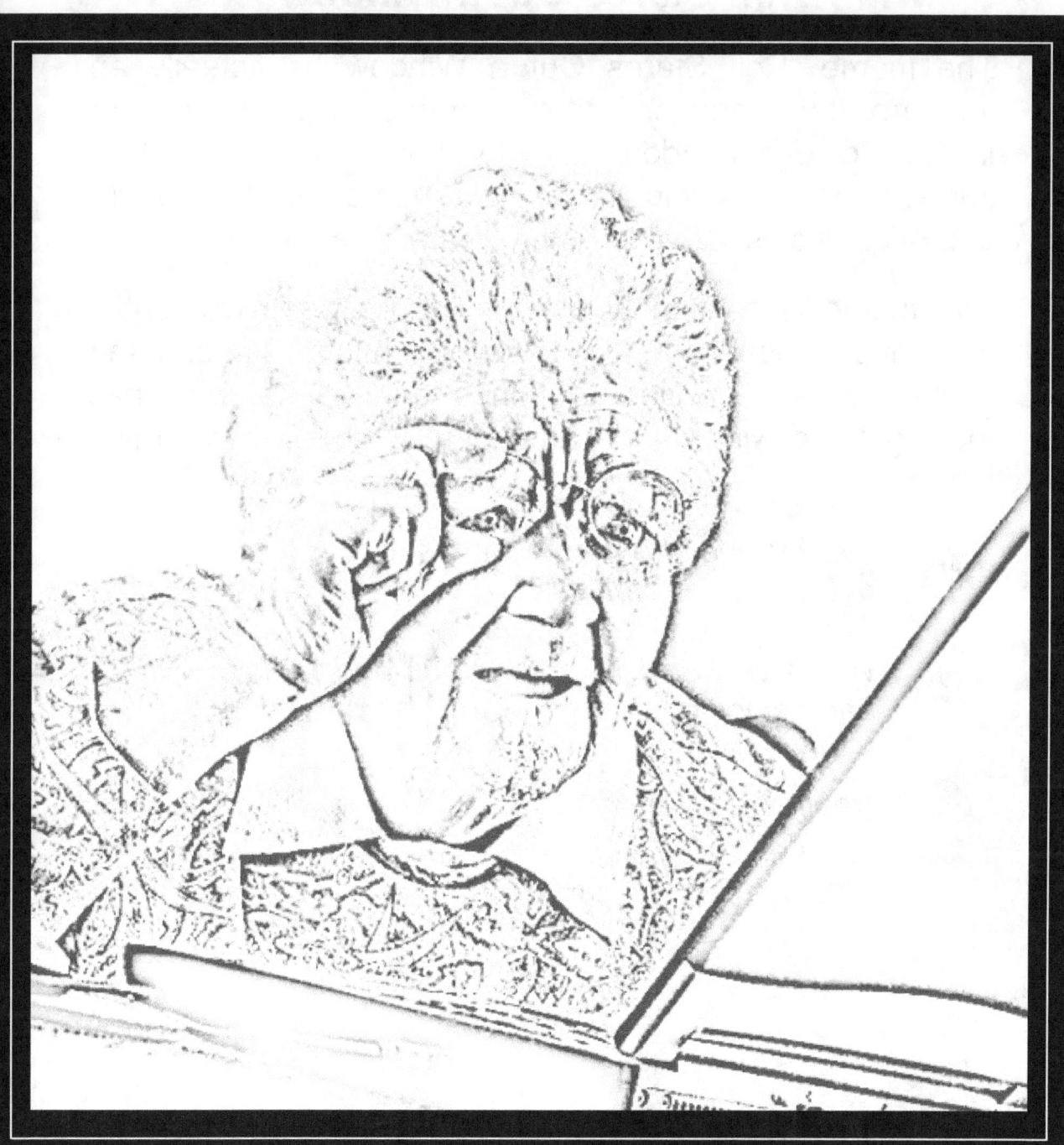

M e m e o l o g y

Rolf Stares Out a Window

The meme "Rolf Stares Out a Window" is actually an image of the character Rolf gazing through his shed door in the 'Ed, Edd n Eddy' episode 'Will Work for Ed'. This image began mass circulation as a meme in 2018 though, the original episode aired many years before in 2001.

The meme is commonly used to depict deep existential thought or critical analysis. However, it has also been used simply to call attention to things one might see while looking out a window- because the internet is weird like that…..

 Me thinking about how there's a "d" in "fridge" but not in "refrigerator".

 When you Google song lyrics and realize you've been singing nonsense for 3 years.

 People really out here just eating well done steak.

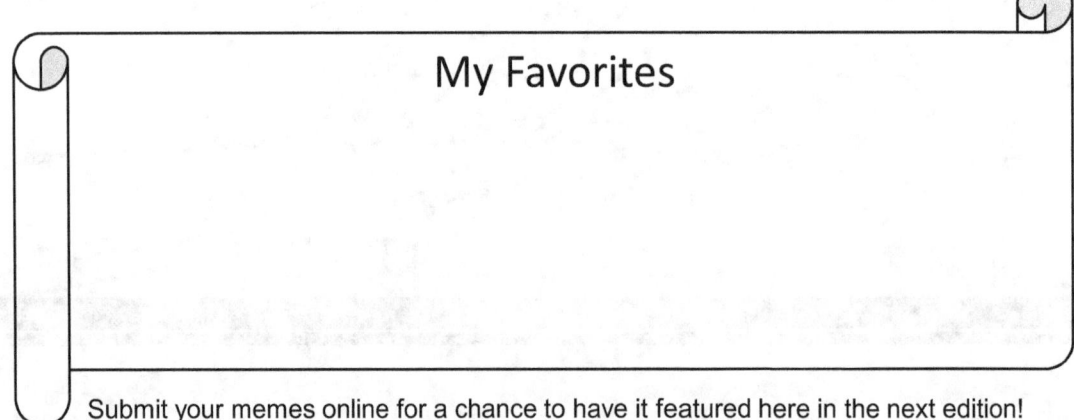

My Favorites

Submit your memes online for a chance to have it featured here in the next edition!

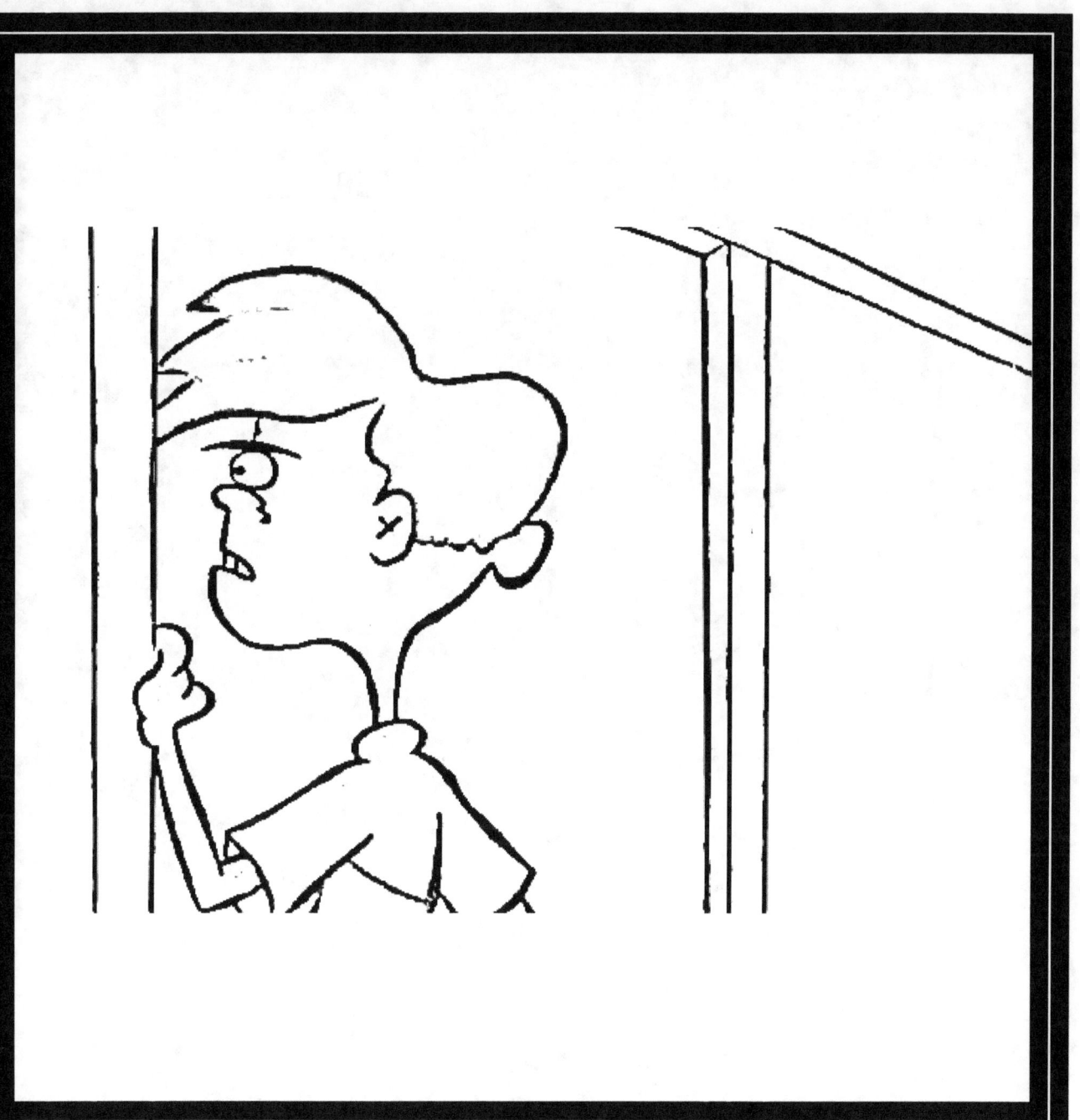

I hope you loved this book as much as we loved creating it! If you did, could you please do us a huge favor and leave a review about your experience on Amazon.

If you were expecting something more, or different, we would love to hear from you so that we can incorporate your ideas and feedback into future books.

To keep up with us and stay up to date on future editions of Memeology: follow us on Facebook, Twitter, Instagram, or Pinterest, or—better yet—head to **MemeColoring.com** and sign up for our VIP List for exclusive deals and early access to the next edition.

And don't forget to upload the memes you create. Tag us for a chance to have your jokes featured in the next edition of Memeology!

 @MemeColoring

 @MemeColoring

 @MemeColoring

 @MemeColoringBooks

#MemeColoring #Memeology #Memes